BUDDHA IN THE PALM
OF YOUR HAND

BUDDHA
IN THE PALM
OF YOUR HAND

Ösel Tendzin

Foreword by Chögyam Trungpa

Edited by Donna Holm

SHAMBHALA
BOULDER & LONDON   1982

SHAMBHALA PUBLICATIONS, INC.
1920 13th Street
Boulder, Colorado 80302

Distributed in the United States by Random House
and in Canada by Random House of Canada Ltd.
Distributed in the United Kingdom by Routledge & Kegan Paul Ltd.,
London and Henley-on-Thames

Printed in the United States of America.

9 8 7 6 5 4 3 2
First Edition

Library of Congress Cataloging in Publication Data
Tendzin, Ösel, 1943-
    Buddha in the palm of your hand.

    Includes index.
    1. Spiritual life (Buddhism) 2. Buddhism—
Doctrines. I. Title.
BQ5660.T46   294.3'4448   81-84450
ISBN 0-87773-223-X (pbk.)   AACR2
ISBN 0-394-70889-X (Random House : pbk.)

CONTENTS

ILLUSTRATIONS

COVER *Ka.* Tibetan seal script for the word "ka," meaning "command." This is the personal seal of the Vajra Regent Ösel Tendzin.

FRONTISPIECE *Buddha Shakyamuni.* This 9th-century Indian (Kashmir) bronze statue depicts the Buddha in teaching mudra. *Courtesy of the Virginia Museum.*

PAGE 26 Calligraphy by Vajracarya the Venerable Chögyam Trungpa, Rinpoche. The inscription reads:
If you know "Not" and have discipline,
Patience will arise along with exertion.
Then the ultimate "No" is attained,
And you are victorious over the maras of the setting sun.
Photograph by George Holmes and Blair Hansen.

PAGE 50 The bodhisattva *Chandraprabha.* This is a photo-diagrammatic representation of the famous eighth-century Japanese bronze statue in the Yakushiji monastery at Nara. *Courtesy Lokesh Chandra. Photograph by George Holmes and Blair Hansen.*

PAGE 76 Jetsün Milarepa (1040-1123). The chief disciple of Marpa, Milarepa is renowned for his songs of devotion and realization. *Courtesy of the Etnografiska Museet, Stockholm.*

PAGE 110 Vajracarya the Venerable Chögyam Trungpa, Rinpoche and Vajra Regent Ösel Tendzin. *Photograph by Liza Matthews.*

PAGE 113 *Four-Armed Mahakala.* Mahakalas are the wrathful protectors of the dharma. This statue is reputed to have belonged to Nagarjuna, the famous Indian master of the second century A.D., who founded the Madhyamaka school. *Photograph by George Holmes and Blair Hansen.*

To His Holiness the Sixteenth Gyalwa Karmapa, Rangjung Rikpe Dorje, whose buddha activity caused the sun of dharma to shine throughout the world; and to the Vidyadhara, the Eleventh Trungpa Tulku, the Venerable Chögyam Trungpa, Rinpoche, my root guru, the one who showed me the way.

ACKNOWLEDGMENTS

EARLY IN 1980, HAVING BEEN REQUESTED by students to publish a book, the Vajra Regent Ösel Tendzin decided to undertake such a project. He was encouraged and supported in this venture by Vajracarya the Venerable Chögyam Trungpa, Rinpoche, as well as by Samuel Bercholz, President and Editor-in-Chief of Shambhala Publications.

The initial research for material for this manuscript began in the spring of that year, using as source material transcripts of talks that had been given by the Vajra Regent throughout the United States over a three-year period from 1977 to 1980. In editing these talks, every effort was made to preserve the original flavor of the Vajra Regent's teaching style, while at the same time rendering the talks into literary form.

The final draft of the manuscript was a collaborative effort of the author, the editor, and Carolyn Rose Gimian, the Editor-in-Chief of Vajradhatu. The collaborative process of finalizing the manuscript was an invaluable experience, and we owe the Vajra Regent our heartfelt thanks for his patience, perseverance, and continual guidance in clarifying our understanding of this material.

We would also like to express our thanks to David I. Rome; the Loppön, Lodrö Dorje Holm; Reginald A. Ray, Chairman of the Buddhist Studies Department of Naropa Institute; and Larry Mermelstein, Executive Director of the Nalanda Translation Committee, for their careful reading of the final manuscript.

Special thanks are due to Sarah Levy of the Vajradhatu Editorial Department, who copy-edited the final manuscript and made many invaluable suggestions as to its revision.

We would also like to thank the Nalanda Translation Committee for the translation from the Tibetan of "The Story of Red Rock Agate Valley" that appears in Part III of this book.

Special thanks are due to the directors and staff of Rocky Mountain Dharma Center, who hosted the Vajra Regent on several occasions during the preparation of the manuscript. Their hospitality and support tremendously facilitated this work. We would also like to express our gratitude to the many volunteers who cooked, cleaned, babysat, typed, ran errands, and in general provided the environment in which this book could be produced.

Finally, we would like to thank the staff of Shambhala Publications for their continued support of this project.

The particular insight and skillfulness that characterize the teachings of the Vajra Regent are presented here in a direct and powerful manner. We hope that this book will not only inspire those who are searching for a genuine and profound path, but also deepen the understanding of those already familiar with the buddhadharma.

Donna Holm
Editor

PROCLAIMING THE LIVING STRENGTH OF THE PRACTICE LINEAGE

IN ORDER TO CREATE A CIVILIZED WORLD, it is very important for one person to trust another. Furthermore, it is very important to impart the wisdom of one human being to another and to trust that wisdom at the same time, knowing that it is immaculate, pure, good, accurate, no nonsense.

In the twentieth century, we talk about democracy, individualism, personal heroism, and all kinds of things like that. While all of those ideals are excellent in one sense, they are the creation of a culture that does not appreciate arduous and long training in a traditional discipline. Throwing away tradition and wisdom that have been developed through many centuries is like tossing the extraordinary exertion and sacrifice that human beings have made out of the window, like dirty socks. This is certainly not the way to maintain the best of human society.

While much of Europe was still quite primitive, tantric Buddhism was flourishing in India. At that time in India, people were less savage. They practiced purification and learned how to treat each other as brothers. Needless to say, such human wisdom evolved by means of compassion and love of the world—love of humanity, animals, plants, flowers, and all the rest. Lord Buddha's message goes along with that: If you feel bad about somebody, don't destroy him; take such bad aggression onto yourself, as if you were in that other person's place.

Thus the tradition of exchanging oneself for others was developed by the Lord Buddha.

In this little book, my Regent, Ösel Tendzin, has discussed the principles of the attainment of enlightenment, that is, human decency and human wakefulness. No self-proclaimed wisdom exists in his writings. Ösel Tendzin reflects here only the study and training he has gone through with my personal guidance. These are the identical teachings that I received in the same way from my teacher, Jamgön Kongtrül of Sechen. So everything in this book is according to the tradition. I would certainly suggest that readers pay a great deal of attention to this work that my Regent has produced.

As members of the Practice Lineage of Tibetan Buddhism, our path and goal are to tame our ego-centered mind, which consists of passion, aggression, and ignorance. As a student and child of mine, Ösel Tendzin has developed his natural ability to respond to the teachings of egolessness. He not only intellectually comprehends these teachings, but he has actually practiced and trained himself in this way. Although I would not say Ösel Tendzin is an enlightened person, he is one of the greatest examples of a practitioner who has followed the command of the Buddha and his guru and the tradition of the Practice Lineage.

Many Oriental advisors have said to me, "Do not make an Occidental your successor; they are not trustworthy." With the blessing of His Holiness the 16th Gyalwa Karmapa, and through working with Ösel Tendzin as my Regent, I have come to the conclusion that anybody who possesses tathagatagarbha is worthy of experiencing enlightenment. Moreover, Ösel Tendzin is my prime student. He has been able to commit himself and learn thoroughly the teachings of vajrayana. I have worked arduously in training him as my best student and foremost leader, and His Holiness Karmapa has confirmed his Regency. With His Holiness' blessing, Ösel Tendzin should hold his title and the sanity of the enlightened lineage. He is absolutely capable of imparting the message of buddhadharma to the rest of the world.

I am extraordinarily happy and joyous that my Regent has made his talks available in the form of a book. This work should be tremendously beneficial to those who would like to follow the path of enlightenment and the Practice Lineage of the Kagyü Tradition.

> Dragon thunders:
> Rainclouds
> Lightning
> Power
> Strength.
> Warrior proclaims:
> Gentle
> Excellent.
> Fruits grow and taste delicious.
> As buddha nature blossoms,
> The world has no regrets
> But experiences the dharma
> And rejoices in the Great Eastern Sun.
> Let us wake as buddha!

Vajracarya the Venerable Chögyam Trungpa, Rinpoche
Boulder, Colorado
16 December 1981

INTRODUCTION

As human beings, we spend most of our lives believing in a myth. We have heard that it is human nature to be bound by anger and fear, hatred and jealousy. We have heard all our lives that it is "only human" to take care of ourselves first. Although it is extremely painful to think of ourselves in such a negative way, it is convenient to believe that myth. At some point or other, most of us just shrug our shoulders and say, "That's the way it is." For although we often feel ashamed of ourselves and our fellow human beings, we feel helpless to change what seems to be inevitable.

Some people might go to great lengths to try to eliminate their fear. But in attempting to do so, they create other myths—the myth of self-sacrifice or the myth of the super hero. However, these approaches only breed further confusion and aggression, because they are based on a fundamental misunderstanding of our nature. Actually, we are stunned by the aggression we see in the world. Unless we have become totally numb and insensitive, we feel sadness when someone is hurt, we feel pity for those who suffer. But we are caught between feeling such sadness and wanting to protect ourselves.

The Buddha taught that all of us have the intelligence and sensitivity to conquer our fear. He taught that we are tender-hearted human beings, who possess a basic goodness. According to the Buddha, if we possess any human nature at all, it is this basic goodness, and by realizing this goodness in ourselves, we

1

can overcome doubt and hesitation. We can actually dissolve the myths about ourselves, conquer our fear, and attain enlightenment. This kind of conquering does not involve force; it relies on gentleness. Only gentle beings can produce a gentle world.

The path of the Buddha is indestructible. People like ourselves who wonder how to make sense out of this life can only benefit by hearing and practicing this ancient and noble tradition. However, following the Buddha's path does take discipline and effort. If we apply discipline and effort and follow the path with a clear mind and a pure heart, it can only lead to a full realization of our basic goodness; it can only lead to unsurpassable, great enlightenment. We are skeptical, no doubt, that such a possibility exists for us. We are fearful, no doubt, that we are too late. We are hopeful, no doubt, that we are just in time.

This book is meant to give a concise and simple outline of the Buddhist path as taught by the Kagyü lineage of Tibet. It is my intention to present a practical way of relating to what some people have considered to be a complicated and unreachable philosophy. Buddhist practice is beyond philosophy; it is a pure and useful teaching. We should not equate purity with Utopian ideals, nor should we understand "useful" to mean utilitarian. These teachings are simple truth, and their power is that they can be applied immediately to our everyday life and the world we live in.

The great teachers of the Kagyü lineage have said that by practicing, you can actually deliver Buddha into the palm of your hand. This is not meant as a boast, but as a declaration of truth. The imagery of the phrase "delivering Buddha into the palm of your hand" is quite literal. It means that you can achieve enlightenment. Buddha refers to awakened mind. The palm of your hand is the gentle resting place of enlightenment, the seat of awakened mind that you already possess. And Buddha can be delivered there by following the instructions of your guru. So delivering Buddha into the palm of your hand means receiving teachings from your guru, practicing them, and taking your place as an awakened being.

In our tradition, teachings are handed down personally from teacher to student. This is called *lineage*. Delivering Buddha into the palm of your hand points out the reality of lineage: it refers to the unending possibility for the transmission of awakened mind to occur. This transmission transcends racial and cultural boundaries. Buddha's mind was not an Indian mind; my guru's mind is not a Tibetan mind; my mind is not an American mind. As a person born and raised in the West, I can say without a doubt that the Buddha's transmission of how to attain enlightenment is applicable to all human beings.

This material is based on the oral instructions given to me personally by my root guru, Vajracarya the Venerable Chögyam Trungpa, Rinpoche, the Eleventh Trungpa Tulku. These instructions were presented to me in a precise form, and I am delighted by the opportunity to present them to others. If I have made any errors, it is purely my fault and not the fault of the teachings. If I have said anything of benefit, it is purely due to the kindness of my teacher.

This is a traditional presentation of the stages of the path. It was not written in order to convert anyone, but to communicate what I know according to what I have been taught and what I have experienced. I offer it as a humble expression of one who has merely begun. My clear desire is for all of us to transcend pettiness and attain the complete enlightenment of a buddha. As far as I can see, there is no real distinction between one human being and another, apart from our idiosyncrasies—and even those are not as problematic as we think they are. I trust that what I have said in this book will help to illuminate that basic fact.

May this book help to eliminate the confusion of beings like myself who, due to carelessness, have forgotten the noble path. No matter who we are, we can attain the ultimate good.

When I met my guru, I saw the rugged power of a
   clear mind.
I fell effortlessly into the open path.
Living under the white umbrella of the compassionate ones,
I remain continually grateful.

PART I

The path of meditation is the way to achieve freedom from confusion by transforming that confusion into wisdom.

ONE

PROVISIONS FOR THE JOURNEY

THROUGHOUT HISTORY THERE HAS ALWAYS BEEN an appreciation of that which is ultimately good and wholesome. The *buddhadharma,* the teachings of the Buddha, provides a way to realize that ultimate good. In this book we propose to study these teachings as transmitted by the gurus of the Kagyü lineage of Tibet. Because their realization and understanding have been based on personal experience, the teachings of their tradition continue to be fresh and alive; they are available to all of us right now. The message of this tradition is how to cultivate enlightened mind.

The motivation to cultivate enlightened mind begins as a vague impulse to achieve something. That vague signal leads us to search for an answer to the fundamental question of who and what we are. Our impulse to search, our longing to achieve, contains the seed of enlightened mind.

What is enlightened mind? According to the Buddhist teachings, enlightened mind is not manufactured. It is not a result of causes nor an accumulation of events; it is not an addition to what already exists. Enlightened mind has no birth and no death. It is without preoccupation, fear, expectation, or disappointment. That state of mind already exists in us; it is intrinsic to all human beings. Without any doubt, each one of us can experience it. That is our basic ground: our mind, as it is, is sufficient to realize the awakened state.

If that is the case, then what needs to be cultivated? The awakened state of mind is habitually obscured by ignorance; therefore it is necessary to cultivate the discipline that can illuminate our true nature. When we lift the veil of ignorance, awakened mind shines by itself.

We might ask, "How do you know there is an awakened state of mind? Can you prove that ignorance exists? Can you prove that enlightenment exists?" These questions express our general concern about our state of mind, about whether we feel good or bad or whether we are right or wrong. They are a manifestation of natural inquisitiveness. Because we are fundamentally open and awake, we are inquisitive; and our inquisitive mind is constantly questioning or searching.

According to the buddhadharma, the proper way to use inquisitiveness is to practice the discipline of meditation. We must constantly apply the technique of meditation practice in order to wear down our habitual tendency to ignore our basic state of mind. Meditative discipline brings about the realization that both ignorance and inquisitiveness come from the original ground of enlightened mind, which is unobstructed and has no allegiance to whatever occurs. That original mind is like a vast, open field, which is beyond success or failure, beyond good or bad.

These teachings are meant to give an outline of what is real and true. If enlightened mind were not already there, we would have no way to begin. The Kagyü lineage, in particular, emphasizes that all of us have basic intelligence, the spark of wisdom. Glimpses of the awakened state of mind occur in our ordinary experience. This is what makes it possible for us to journey on the path to enlightenment.

There are two aspects of this path: practice and study. Practice is the most important, because only through direct, personal experience can we attain realization. In fact, the Kagyü lineage is called the Practice Lineage. The second aspect, study or intellectual understanding of the teachings, illuminates our practice and confirms our intuitive experience. Those two, practice and study, are the provisions for our journey.

Having a proper attitude towards journey is essential. If we make a journey properly, then everything we encounter is considered part of it. We are fully involved in the process of journeying rather than being fixated on our destination. We are not looking for quick solutions, but we are willing to be open, precise, and thorough in relating with ourselves as well as all the facets of our environment—the weather, the scenery, the landmarks, and the obstacles or sidetracks along the way.

As we begin our journey, the biggest obstacle that we encounter is materialism. Materialism in general is the ego-centered notion of possessing things for oneself. Physical materialism is the accumulation of material comforts; psychological materialism is the accumulation of philosophies, ideologies, or psychological theories. But the most extreme and dangerous form of materialism is spiritual materialism.

Before we are even attracted to spiritual materialism, we have already become dissatisfied with physical and psychological comforts. Spiritual materialism is based on trying to possess the highest spiritual state, trying to have the best meditative experience. We adopt a spiritual disguise in order to mask our own fear and clinging; we convert spiritual teachings into personal territory. We smother any spark of intelligence, and in the process, we deceive ourselves and produce spiritual fraud. We may even go so far as to encourage others to follow us in our deception by capitalizing on their confusion and encouraging a "herd instinct."

9

In entering the path to enlightenment, we are beginning the process of transforming confusion into wisdom. But in order to make this journey, we must first acknowledge that we are confused and that our environment is chaotic. Beyond that, we must understand that chaos and confusion are perpetuated because we do not have the training to see things as they are.

The only way to begin our journey is to work with confusion. Looking into confusion is the opposite of spiritual materialism. Adopting spiritual materialism, we would like to disregard confusion and immediately embrace our own idea of enlightenment. We would like to believe we can accomplish in three days what should involve our whole life. In trying to sidestep confusion, trying to get around it, we miss something very dear and precious. In fact, we miss our own wisdom. Therefore it is best to begin simply, by taking a fresh look at our world and our experience.

TWO

A STRAIGHTFORWARD VIEW

WHEN WE LOOK AT OUR LIFE in a straightforward way, we see that everything is marked by impermanence, or transitoriness. Anything that is born will eventually die. The phenomenal world and our bodies are subject to birth, life, decay, and death. It is the same with our thoughts and emotions. We feel happy and that lasts for a while, and then that happiness might change into sadness or depression. We cannot even hang on to our belief in consciousness as an eternal principle. If we look carefully, we see that even consciousness is purely a collection of mental events that having been brought together, eventually disperse.

Since the experience of impermanence is all-pervasive, there is nothing that we can grasp and hold on to and say, "This lasts forever." We are left with a sense of groundlessness. That experience is the discovery of egolessness. Because we are confused, we base our perceptions on an idea of ourselves as a permanent entity. That so-called permanent entity is known as "ego." But there is no permanent self or ego—there are simply mental events, which in themselves are impermanent.

When we try to find out who we are, we cannot come up with anything. There is nothing concrete or real or solid that we can call "me" or "myself." We might think we are our body, but we know the body decays. We might think we are our thought process, but we know that thoughts constantly change. We might think we are our memories, but they come and go, they fade away and return. So we cannot depend on any of that as a

11

constant reference point to prove that we exist. Even when we try to pin down who it is that perceives impermanence, we get completely dumbfounded. Our intuition and our knowledge cannot be attached to anything. There is no permanent witness to any event.

Not seeing clearly the truth of impermanence and egoless-ness, we suffer. We suffer when we experience change; we suffer because we do not know who we are. We have a feeling of separation between who we think we are and our body, our thoughts, our emotions, and our environment, and that pro-vokes continual ambivalence and anxiety. In refusing to acknowledge our basic anxiety, we become numb. That numb-ness takes the form of believing in a permanent self or ego. But the more we cling to the belief in a self, the more pain and alienation we feel.

According to the Buddhist teachings, that perpetuation of suffering need not happen. We do not have to create boundaries in order to define ourselves. It is possible to look at our lives in a more straightforward way. We can experience impermanence, egolessness, and suffering simply, without having to create a fortification called "I." We can glimpse the possibility of uprooting our confusion. At that point, because we see the reality of impermanence, egolessness, and suffering, we get fed up and disgusted with repeating the same pain over and over again. This is a very positive step. Our revulsion and nausea bring the recognition that this human birth, which is so very tenuous, is very precious at the same time. We realize that death can come at any minute; we have no idea when we are going to die. Therefore, we feel we must find a way out of our confusion.

The path of meditation is the way to achieve freedom from confusion by transforming that confusion into wisdom. Medita-tion practice does not introduce the notion of a higher being who will rescue us, nor does it propose that attaining a higher consciousness will save us. It works with what we have right now: our perceptions, our memories, our emotions, our thoughts. Meditation practice is the process of being awake to what is. What is needed is commitment.

THREE

THE LANDSCAPE

WE SHOULD UNDERSTAND THAT THE CAUSE of confused existence, or *samsara*, is the struggle to survive. We hope that we will continue to survive, and we fear that we won't. Hope and fear play off each other all the time and create what we know as everyday life. Those emotions arise because seemingly there is a threat to our continued existence. Not being able to remember the moment we were born and not knowing when we are going to die, we live with constant uncertainty. We avoid speculating about the moment of death, and trying to remember our birth seems impossible—so we continue our struggle to survive. We hope to achieve ultimate, everlasting security, and this keeps us continually preoccupied.

This preoccupation is fueled by what are traditionally known as the *three poisons:* passion, aggression, and ignorance. These confused emotions are the basic energy of ego. If we feel that something will help us to survive, we try to attract or hold or possess it. That is passion. If we think that something threatens our survival, we try to repel, intimidate, or destroy it. That is aggression. If we feel indifferent, lazy, or dull, that is ignorance. The momentum of passion, aggression, and ignorance builds until the energy produces different styles of preoccupation, hallucinatory worlds, which are known as the *six realms*. The experience in each of these realms is overwhelming suffering.

Sometimes we create a habitual existence in which everything is predictable, so that there is no need to relate with the uncompromising quality of pain. This particular attitude describes what is known as the animal realm, or the consciousness like that of an animal. This style of imprisonment is based on ignorance. The quality of our experience in this realm is a kind of numbness and lack of humor. Like animals, we are slaves to the seasons and the environment. We just plod along, ignoring the implications of our experiences. We are born, grow old, and die; our family, friends, and associates come and go. Life is taken for granted. We experience disappointment and achievement, but never with any enthusiasm. Day turns into night; weeks become months; months become years. We take everything literally because we are afraid to speculate on the meaning of our existence.

Then perhaps we dream of other possibilities, and we become seized by a sense of hunger. We think our predictable life is too limited, and we want to discover a more interesting and satisfying world. But our search already has a sense of hunger attached to it. We feel starved and we carry our starvation with us everywhere. This is the realm of the hungry ghosts, which is motivated by passion. The notion of a ghost here is that of a phantom in an unfamiliar world. We are out of our own environment and looking for something different. What we find appears to be delightful, but it never really satisfies us. We feel we have finally found a delicious world, a rich world, and we try to devour it. The sense of being starved pushes us to try to eat tremendous amounts, but when we do, we vomit. Then we feel hungry and have to eat again. No matter how much we eat or how often, no matter how much richness we experience, nothing can remove our sense of hunger, our sense of poverty. We are still trapped in the hope of achieving ultimate satisfaction.

When sensual delights prove to be unsatisfactory, we begin to feel we should transcend the problems and limitations of desire. We think: "Perhaps if I get into the realm of thought, I can achieve a sense of security. Philosophical pleasure doesn't help that much; however, spiritual pleasure might bring ultimate fulfillment. Perhaps the most sublime thing would be to have a mind that cannot be disturbed. The best mind would be cloud-like, spacelike—limitless, untouchable, and unshakable." These thoughts are delightful and, in fact, very exciting. We become enthused by the idea that we could actually dwell in celestial space with uninterrupted pleasure and security. We could possess ultimate victory, power, and discipline. We could achieve continual bliss by becoming a spiritual being.

All the energy of our search for security is now channeled into developing a sophisticated mental world. We become preoccupied with the contemplation of limitless space and cosmic principles. This is called the realm of the gods. The experience of this realm is characterized by concentration or absorption, which is actually a more subtle form of ignorance. By concentrating our mind, we create a kind of euphoria or trance. We become hypnotized by our own mental energy. We assume the posture of one who knows the heavens, one who is completely in touch with the cosmos. We experience power and stability, and we feel we have reached our destination.

Feeling we have reached the highest state where nothing can touch us, we begin to relax, believing we no longer have to struggle. At first this feels wonderful, but after a while we notice a subtle change in energy, and we become slightly uncomfortable. We try to adjust to the change, but any little movement or deviation from that sense of limitless existence is frightening. When fear comes into the picture, we begin to doubt our accomplishment; we think that maybe we missed the point

16

altogether. Then we start to lose confidence in our power to concentrate. Paranoia and aggression begin to creep in, and we enter the realm of the jealous gods.

In this realm, as we become more anxious and upset, we start looking everywhere for the cause of our discomfort. But we cannot look everywhere at once, and that increases our paranoia and our sense of being victimized. We become highly defensive and feel we must not let anyone see that we have fallen from our lofty seat, our state of grace. We try to act relaxed, but we feel overwhelmingly irritated by the constant pressure to secure our world and maintain our secret. We no longer possess any composure, and we blame others for our misfortune. We become jealous of anyone who seems to be better off than we are. We are sure there is some further knowledge that would solve our problems. At the same time we feel ourselves sinking faster and faster from the heights, and we become more and more afraid.

Eventually we become so fearful that our life becomes a nightmare. Everything and everyone we encounter is horrific. Our fear becomes so exaggerated that even simple sense experiences become extremely threatening and painful: a drink of water becomes poison; a pleasant, sunny day becomes unbearably hot. The world becomes a complete and total threat. We have descended into the realm of hell, which is marked by continual anger and hatred. There seems to be no way out. In fact, the more we try to escape, the more torturous the nightmare becomes.

In all of the five realms we have just described, we never see the cause of our continual pain. Our state of mind is so solid that we are not even aware that we are confused. In only one of the six realms, the human realm, can we experience any possibility of freedom from our otherwise endless imprisonment in hallucinatory worlds. This possibility arises when there is a gap or break in the intensity of our pain. Such a break allows us to glimpse the confused nature of our existence; it allows us to relate with our pain. In terms of conventional logic, when we discover pain we hope there is an alternative. In terms of buddhadharma, since pain is the nature of existence, we realize we should examine it thoroughly. The opportunity to do so arises only in the human realm.

FOUR

CONSIDERING THE TRUTH

THE HUMAN REALM IS THE ONLY REALM in which we can unravel the thread of confusion and attain enlightenment. The Buddhist teachings speak of human existence as precious because it provides the working basis for that attainment. Why is this so? Each form of existence, or realm, is marked by a particular neurotic emotion. The neurotic emotion of the human realm is passion, or desire—but it is a less poverty-stricken form of passion than that associated with the hungry ghost realm. The passion of the human realm is longing rather than hunger. This longing is what leads us to search for a spiritual path.

As human beings, we generally believe that desire is good and healthy and, in fact, essential. We think if we were utterly without desire we would cease to exist. Ordinarily, desire implies the possibility of fulfillment, of possessing the object of our desires. But actually, as long as there is desire there can be no fulfillment. Accomplishing our goals never really satisfies us. This is because the object of desire is always the projection of ego, and therefore has no essential reality.

When we start to realize this, we become disappointed. Our disappointment becomes so vivid that we feel disgusted with confused existence, and we are drawn to looking deeper into our life. We begin to question whether trying to fulfill our desires is all there is to life. We ask ourselves, "What is the meaning of life? What am I doing? Where am I going?" It doesn't matter how successful we have been in our endeavors. If we have the honesty to penetrate the veneer, the outward display of our life, we realize how wretched we actually feel. Although our feelings of disgust and wretchedness are irritating and painful, at the same time they are clearly auspicious. They prompt us to search for a spiritual path and allow us to go beyond our usual preoccupations and defenses.

In the other realms there is no possibility of intelligent doubt, of actually thinking, "Does it have to be this way? Is it possible that I am taking the wrong approach altogether?" The intensity of pain in those realms is so overwhelming that there is no gap in experience. There is no time to wonder about or question what is going on. Habitual patterns are so vivid and claustrophobic that the thought of seeking enlightenment never occurs. Only in the human realm can we conceive of such a thought, and that thought comes out of the experience of disappointment. At that point we are able to hear the noble doctrine of the Buddha. In that way, the desire of the human realm becomes a useful tool for attaining enlightenment. Without such longing, merely being born in the human realm is not likely to lead to liberation. It becomes just another stage in our continual journey through the six realms.

The doctrine of the Buddha begins with the teaching of the *four noble truths*. The four noble truths show the path of liberation in the human realm. They are called *noble* because they liberate us from confusion. They are *true* because they are not based on speculation, nor are they contrasted with falsehood. They are simply the statement of what is. Merely hearing the teaching of the four noble truths can cut the speed and intensity of our preoccupations. Listening to the Buddha's description of the nature of confused existence and the nature of the path to liberation, we begin to develop a new perspective. That perspective is the perspective of enlightenment.

The first noble truth is that suffering is the nature of existence. All of existence—all of the six realms, including the human realm—is marked by suffering. The second noble truth describes the origin of suffering. The origin or cause of suffering is craving to maintain a self, ego. That craving gives rise to conflicting emotions and *karma*, the inevitability of cause and effect that brings about the continuous cycle of birth and death in the six realms. The third noble truth proclaimed by the Buddha declares that there is an end, a cessation, to suffering. When the Buddha talked about the cessation of suffering, he was not talking about pain becoming happiness or pleasure. Cessation is the end of struggle and confusion. The fourth noble truth is that there is a path that leads to the cessation of struggle and the attainment of enlightenment. The primary discipline of this path is the practice of meditation.

This path was practiced by the Buddha himself, and has been transmitted from that time to the present day. It has been handed down from teacher to student through the ages, uninterruptedly and without corruption. By hearing, contemplating and practicing the Buddha's teachings, confidence starts to grow in us. This confidence is not blind faith based on ignorance or wishful thinking. It is the beginning of real conviction based on personal experience. We begin to actually appreciate the preciousness of our human birth.

FIVE

THE RESERVOIR OF COMMITMENT

IN ORDER TO BE A PRACTITIONER of the buddhadharma, it is necessary to recognize and develop three types of faith. Faith means the confidence in our intelligence that enables us to practice meditation and understand the four noble truths.

The first type of faith or confidence is called *trusting confidence*. This trust is based on understanding the Buddha's teaching of cause and effect, or karma. Trust in the teaching of karma is the starting point for any practitioner of the dharma. Karma is not particularly mystical; it is the simple law of cause and effect. Karma begins with the ignorance of clinging to a self. Attempting to maintain a self creates a continual chain of volitional action based on impulse and expressed through body, speech, and mind. Our present circumstances are the result of volitional actions in the past; our future circumstances depend on volitional actions in the present.

Thus karma, or volitional action, is motivated by confusion— that is, by belief in a self or ego. This confusion ultimately results in birth in the six realms. Virtuous actions produce a favorable birth in a higher realm—the realm of the gods, jealous gods, or humans. Aggressive or degraded actions produce birth in a lower realm—the realm of hell-beings, animals, or hungry ghosts. The aim of the practitioner is to cut this chain reaction entirely by means of the practice of meditation.

The second type of confidence is called *longing confidence*. This is the recognition that enlightenment is possible. Having realized the possibility of liberation from confusion, a sense of longing or eagerness to attain it naturally develops.

The third type of confidence is called *lucid confidence.* An understanding of the misery of confused existence and the truth of karma, together with a longing to free ourselves from samsara, brings clear vision. We realize that the three jewels—the *Buddha,* the *dharma,* and the *sangha*—are the means to liberation. This is lucid confidence. It is the motivation to take the refuge vow, the first formal commitment that we make as practitioners.

Taking refuge in the three jewels means acknowledging, to begin with, that we are alone and that being alone is itself an expression of human dignity. We discover that there is no alternative to working with ourselves. There is no time left to be a spiritual consumer, constantly comparing prices in a supermarket of different spiritual disciplines, window shopping, glancing through catalogues. There are no promises that can be bought or bargained for in the confused world. Those activities can only produce further suffering.

When we make that discovery we become inspired to take a very definite and sure step: we commit ourselves to the path of the awakened one, the Buddha, by taking the vow of refuge. That is the first step in transforming our chaotic world into a sane world. Taking refuge in the three jewels is a statement of our commitment to ourselves. We formally acknowledge that the process of transforming confusion into wisdom has begun and will continue until we are freed from the interminable suffering of samsara. This is accomplished by understanding the nature of the three jewels of refuge: the Buddha, the dharma, and the sangha.

Taking refuge in the Buddha means realizing that a human being like ourselves attained enlightenment and, in fact, practitioners have been doing so for over 2,500 years. The basis for our commitment is not the worship of a divine being; it is knowing that we can do precisely as the Buddha himself did. When we take refuge in the Buddha, we understand there is no external savior. The Buddha sat alone and attained enlightenment, and we take refuge in his example. We must do as he did: rely on our own mind, our own exertion, our own practice. That is what we have right now, and that is sufficient.

The second object of refuge is the dharma, that is, the teachings of the Buddha. We take refuge in what the Buddha taught. We acknowledge that the dharma is our basic guideline, our only reference point in working with everything we encounter in our life: our thought processes, emotions, bodily sensations, relationships, and so on. Since the essence of the teachings is contained in the practice of meditation, we commit ourselves wholeheartedly to that discipline when we take refuge in the dharma as path.

The third object of refuge is the sangha, the community of practitioners, spiritual friends, who like ourselves are committed to the path of sanity. Relating with the sangha brings the understanding that our fellow practitioners are making the same journey. The fact that there are other people practicing in the same way provides a lot of encouragement. At the same time there is no sense of dependency. We do not have to lean on our companions. We have genuine respect for the people around us; therefore we would like to create and maintain an environment of sanity for them. That creates tremendous power and sense of community. At the same time we do not forget that our journey is a solitary journey, a lonely journey. When we experience our aloneness in the midst of the sangha, we realize the unique quality of our journey. We reaffirm our commitment to practice because we understand there is no fantasy involved in this path—we must walk on it ourselves.

Taking refuge actually changes the course of history. Waking up to our own decency cuts the chain reaction of endless rebirth in samsara, the six realms. In our lifetime there are very few events that make sense, very few decisions we make that ultimately change our lives. This is one of the few sensible things we can ever do. At the same time, making such a commitment means that we have no choice but to proceed, to move forward towards enlightenment.

ཨེན

no   no

མ་ཐེན

SIX

OVERCOMING HOPE AND FEAR

As a result of realizing the three types of confidence and taking refuge in the three jewels, we begin to appreciate discipline. Having heard the teaching of the four noble truths, we recognize the importance of discipline as the means of liberating ourselves from confusion. The path that leads to enlightenment, as transmitted by the Kagyü lineage, consists of three *yanas*, or vehicles—the *hinayana, mahayana,* and *vajrayana.* The three yanas provide specific disciplines that are suited to the various stages of a student's development.

In the first yana, the hinayana, the practitioner frees himself from confusion by not indulging in degraded or samsaric activity. The goal of this practice is the attainment of *sosor tharpa,* or *individual liberation.* In the second yana, the mahayana, the practitioner vows to attain enlightenment not simply for himself, but for the benefit of others. In the vajrayana, the final stage of the path, when the student has thoroughly prepared the ground through the practices of the previous yanas, he develops the ability to transform confusion into wisdom on the spot.

Traditionally, the attainment of individual liberation in the hinayana is accomplished by practicing the three disciplines: *shila, samadhi,* and *prajna*—right conduct, meditative absorption, and discriminating awareness. Shila is the discipline of not harming oneself or others. Samadhi, meditative absorption, is the practice of unwinding confusion, and prajna is the discriminating awareness that leads to enlightenment.

We could begin with a discussion of shila or, in Tibetan, *tsültrim,* proper action. The discipline of proper action is not to cause harm to oneself or others; and it comes out of disgust at having done so, time and time again. Not harming others does not imply, at this point, helping others. It is not actually possible to help others properly until we stop creating pain for ourselves. So, to begin with, we have to recognize the suffering of our own existence and develop the resolve not to create further pain and confusion for ourselves.

In order to do that, we must develop an attitude of renunciation. Renunciation is generally understood as giving up pleasure, whether it is the pleasure we take in money, food, sex, clothing, or any other worldly activities. This is the common interpretation of renunciation—a kind of deprivation. True renunciation, however, is not particularly involved with the practice of asceticism.

Before attaining enlightenment, the Buddha practiced many different types of asceticism in order to eliminate worldly desires. In order to eliminate craving, he underwent severe fasts; in order to eliminate attachment to his body, he subjected it to extremes of heat and cold; in order to overcome ignorance, he went without sleep; in order to let go of attachment to worldly dwelling places, he meditated every day in a different place. He attained all that his teachers could show him, but he realized he was still not free of ego-clinging. Therefore he abandoned conventional ascetic practices. He realized that if he did not take care of his body, he could not practice meditation; if he could not practice meditation, he could not attain enlightenment. He decided to remain on one spot and eat enough food to sustain his body. He arranged a comfortable seat and devoted himself to simple practice.

Proper renunciation begins with being willing to look at the pollution we create with our desire for personal gain and pleasure. That desire is fueled by hope and fear, the mechanisms of ego's survival. By taking the attitude of renunciation and not succumbing to the desire to perpetuate ego, we free ourselves from our continuous grasping. Thus the discipline of renunciation could be described as a kind of energy conservation. It involves taming the wildness of mind by establishing a neutral ground that is not subject to the rages of hope and fear. That neutral ground is created by the practice of meditation. Since there is no external savior, no means to individual liberation other than working with ourselves, we must practice meditation. We must work with being alone, being by ourselves.

We see the pollution caused by lust, stupidity, greed, envy, and pride, and we see that by not refraining from those actions we cause harm to ourselves and others. When we bring the discipline of renunciation to our practice of meditation, we make a very powerful discovery. We discover that there is tremendous dignity in our human existence. We no longer have to cater to the demands of hope and fear. We realize that we have the strength to be disciplined and the decency to be gentle. That is shila.

The second discipline is samadhi. Samadhi, or meditative absorption, refers to subduing or stilling confusion by means of one-pointed absorption in a meditative technique. Samadhi is developed through the techniques of mindfulness and awareness. As we have said, meditation practice creates a neutral ground, where we can relate simply and directly with our body and our breath and our environment. In that neutral situation, our mental world becomes quite vivid. We witness the newsreel of our lives, our mental autobiography, in memories, discursive thoughts, and emotions. Once we begin to practice, we come home, so to speak. When we visit our family after a long absence, there is a great commotion. All of our relatives are very excited; they haven't seen us in years. Some of them cry; others seem very happy and relaxed; others are brooding—it's quite a show. Coming home in terms of meditation practice is the same. All of our relatives—our mental family of memories, dreams, hopes and fears, what we have been, what we are, what we hope to be—start to speak up, expressing their reaction to having us home.

When a particular thought arises in our mind, we feel excited or sad or panicky. Sometimes we feel like falling asleep; other times we feel so angry that we want to jump up. Occasionally our life story seems like a very vivid and garish cartoon; but at other times we feel like congratulating ourselves on how well we are doing. So confused existence has the quality of spinning around and around, very fast. The practice of meditation gives us the opportunity to be still so that we can see our confused, spinning mind. When that stillness becomes continuous, that is the experience of samadhi.

The third discipline, which is born from the previous two, is known as prajna, discriminating awareness, or knowledge. There are two types of knowledge. The first is conventional knowledge, knowledge based on the accumulation of information, memory, and so on. Biased by ego, we pick and choose what we think is of value. Whatever is pleasing to us is considered a proper object of knowledge, and whatever is painful is considered something to ignore. The second type of knowledge arises from pure, inquisitive mind that has no bias. This is prajna. This type of knowledge does not depend on a knower; therefore it is egoless. Prajna is intuitively felt rather than remembered. It understands the nature of things as they are.

We begin to develop prajna by examining the components of our experience. Is confusion real? Is pain real? Does happiness exist? Is there a state of mind that might be called enlightened? If so, what does that mean? What is mind? What are thoughts and emotions? Prajna examines what is, precisely, without the bias of ego's interpretation. It uncovers knowledge of how our body, speech, and mind function; how the world works; how there is confusion and how there is liberation. More specifically, prajna is the knowledge of how thoughts arise, linger, and fade away; how thoughts, in their vividness, become emotions; how emotions give rise to actions; and how actions produce results. Contemplating in this way liberates us from the intense confusion of the six realms.

SEVEN

CONNECTING WITH THE EARTH

DISGUST WITH SAMSARA LEADS US TO SEEK a discipline that will cut through habitual patterns. We look for a path, a teaching that is not based on accumulating further neurosis and confusion. The discipline that provides the framework for our entire path is the formal practice of sitting meditation. Meditation practice allows us to look at things clearly, and we begin to develop mindfulness. Mindfulness means paying attention to the details of our experience. Without mindfulness, we stumble, we get confused, we lose our way, and there is no possibility of proceeding. When we do not miss the details of our experience, we are awake, alert, and precise.

The practice of mindfulness is common to all Buddhist traditions. Although the techniques may vary slightly, the basic practice is the same. The meditation practice that cultivates mindfulness is known in Sanskrit as *shamatha*, which means dwelling in peace—taming the mind. The Tibetan term for that is *shine*. Peacefulness does not mean numbness or casualness, but rather feeling at home with the natural precision of mind. The practice of shamatha meditation is characterized by expanding rather than focusing on one point. Centralizing everything is a problem because it assumes that everything revolves around "me," "myself." Clinging to the notion of self produces the pain of hope and fear. So shamatha practice is based on letting go of the tightness of self-involvement.

The technique of sitting meditation is very simple: it is the process of becoming one with the breath. It is very important to understand the difference between following the breath and becoming one with the breath. Following the breath involves some kind of witness or watcher, and can actually reinforce the sense of self or ego. Strictly speaking, becoming one with the breath does not involve any kind of witness. Breathing does not need a watcher; it is not self-conscious. The breath goes in and out very naturally. We do not consciously have to try to breathe. So working with the breath is not adding anything particularly new to our experience.

Traditionally, meditation is practiced sitting cross-legged on a cushion of some kind. Sitting on a cushion on the ground is a statement of our connection with earth; that is, we are not fantasizing. We are being realistic and practical. The first thing we do is simply to sit down on our meditation cushion. We relax and take a comfortable posture, upright but not rigid. Correct posture means sitting with our head, shoulders, and spine vertically aligned, but without tension. This posture expresses our wakefulness—we are not asleep or dreaming.

After arranging the proper seat, we rest our hands comfortably on our thighs, palms down. Our eyes are open, and our gaze is directed slightly downward. We do not have to stare fixedly at one point or blur everything into a fuzzy haze, but gently take in the immediate environment.

At that point we become aware of our breath going out. As we do so, we feel the actual physical breath going out—not just a mental picture of the breath. It goes to the end of its journey and dissolves into space. As the breath goes out, it has a particular texture and tone and outward movement. Sometimes it is ragged; sometimes it feels very smooth. Sometimes it is shallow, and other times it is deep or heavy. We should be mindful of the texture of the breath without trying to change it. When the breath dissolves into space, there is a gap. At that moment there is no memory of the meditator. The breath dissolves, there is a gap, and that is followed by the inbreath. The inbreath is not emphasized. It is simply a natural function: our lungs are filling with air. The breath just comes back; then it goes out again. Breath; out; dissolve; gap. That is precisely the process we are working with.

When we begin to meditate, we feel self-conscious. We have an exaggerated sense of ourselves as "the meditator." That is not particularly a problem. However, we should remember that what we are interested in doing is becoming one with the breath. The reason we work with the outbreath is because it has a natural sense of expansion and decentralization, of letting go and going out as opposed to focusing on "this," or "me." There is no one watching the breath go out. There is simply breath going out into space and dissolving.

This process is very important because it brings a sense of leaving this territory, this "I." The practice of meditation awakens the intuitive sense of egolessness. Breath goes out, dissolves into space, and comes back; goes out, dissolves into space, and comes back. By practicing in this way we are eroding the basis of ego. It is so simple that it does not involve any concept at all. In fact, when we say, "going out," "dissolving," and "gap," we are just pointing to how to practice. Individually, we find our way.

Generally speaking, when we begin to practice we think we should become an "ideal" meditator—someone who can follow the technique without being interrupted by thoughts. However, we have a lot of accumulated memories, and the thought process continually churns them up. What do we do with the thoughts that we experience? According to the traditional instructions, when a thought arises, we label it "thinking." It is not said aloud; we just mentally label, "thinking." We might ask, "Isn't that just another thought?" Labeling thinking is merely a reminder to return to the breath. The word "thinking" doesn't mean anything. It marks that moment of awareness when we realize we are thinking rather than being one with the breath.

When we are practicing, following the technique, it dawns on us that we are actually meditating properly. Then we become fascinated by that. In the process of becoming fascinated, we also become self-conscious and start to worry about whether we can maintain our experience of meditation. That immediately opens the door to discursive thoughts because we are again focusing on the notion of ourself as the meditator. We are inviting back all our memories, fantasies, hopes, and fears.

Sometimes that fantasy world seems overwhelming and has the appearance of a private horror show of our own. The point is not to take it too seriously. Just look at it. It doesn't matter whether it is pleasing or not—it is simply "thinking." Labeling thinking is like a sharp knife, which cuts precisely but gently. When we label a thought "thinking," it is not a matter of pushing it away. At the point when we label "thinking," the thought process is cut, on the spot. By doing that, we automatically come right back to the breath.

Bodily sensations are also labeled "thinking." We could say that whenever we are not one with the breath, everything that arises in our practice is labeled "thinking." This includes the itch on our face and the pain in our knees. This does not mean that our posture must be absolutely rigid. If we are so distracted by a particular physical pain that we cannot follow the technique, it is sometimes necessary to adjust our posture.

The practice of meditation makes us very sensitive, not from the point of view of becoming touchy or irritable, but from the point of view of becoming sharp and precise. We become like a needle—very thin and clean, straight and pointed. We pay attention to everything that goes on in our life all the time. Mindfulness throws a spotlight on all our behavior. Since our actions are an echo or mirror image of our state of mind, every gesture is worthy of attention. We begin to see how our behavior affects the world around us and how each little move we make can create chaos. If we fail to see this, we push our way through the world, bumping into each other and stepping on each other's toes. We fail to notice where we are going and what we are doing. Our behavior is haphazard and chaotic, lacking dignity and intelligence because it is based on impulse. Through the practice of meditation we can become gentle and dignified human beings.

Although I have given written instructions on how to meditate, it is necessary not only to read and study the teachings, but also to receive personal instruction from a qualified teacher. It is necessary to have an ongoing relationship with one who has made this journey already. Since the time of the Buddha, meditation practice has been transmitted in this way, personally, from teacher to student.

EIGHT

THE CLEAR ATMOSPHERE

SHAMATHA MEDITATION IS VERY SIMPLE and direct: using the technique of working with the breath and labeling thoughts we begin to see that sensations, thoughts, and emotions are simple events. Things as they are, are simple, good, and direct. They do not need elaboration. In fact, we could say that the cause of chaos and aggression is our tendency to create unnecessary complications. So the more we practice, the more we understand a sense of great simplicity.

The practice of shamatha brings freedom from clutter, from the continual whirlpool of our thought process and our constant sense of anxiety, our sense of being chased by our own emotions and sensations. The introduction of mindfulness into our life is like good, fresh air. We see that it is not necessary to complicate our life. There is no longer any reason to believe in a fantasy of who and what we are. We experience our thought process, our body, our actions, and our environment directly, without having to invent a so-called ego. This freedom from complications brings the experience of unfabricated healthiness, wholesomeness, and goodness.

The discovery of simplicity brings delight in practice. When we first meditate, taking delight in our practice might seem artificial. But genuine delight is not an attitude that we adopt. It is a natural result of the simplicity that comes from mindfulness: seeing things directly and not having to invent a sense of identity is delightful. At the same time, it is impossible to discover such delight unless we have discipline. With discipline, delight in practice becomes a continual process, which regenerates itself and expands without effort. We need discipline to allow that state of mind to unfold.

As we continue to practice, delight and goodness naturally grow beyond the boundaries of simple mindfulness. Because of the basic wholesomeness of shamatha, we experience stability of mind and confidence in our practice. Because our state of wholesomeness is continuous and real, and because our practice is good and solid, we are confident of not falling again and again into a whirlpool of confusion. We have recognized that our thought process is not problematic, and therefore we can relax with our thoughts and emotions and bodily sensations—with whatever occurs in our practice.

Once we begin to relax in practice, flashes of insight occur. This is the beginning of *vipashyana*. Vipashyana is a Sanskrit term that means insight, or clear seeing. The Tibetan term for vipashyana is *lhakthong*. The clear seeing of vipashyana arises out of shamatha. From shamatha we learn that things are very direct: senses, body, thoughts. The experience of shamatha practice teaches us that things are just what they are; therefore we relax in our practice. Mindfulness naturally expands into vipashyana insight, and we begin to notice the atmosphere around our practice. This is called awareness. We begin to look out, expand, and insight occurs spontaneously.

With the insight of vipashyana, we recognize the elements of every situation as being without the bias of ego. We see that our world is a combination of factors that, in themselves, have no particular meaning other than what we attribute to them at each moment. This is the discovery of egolessness: realizing that things have no solid existence. This expansion of insight brings tremendous ventilation, freedom, a spacious attitude. At the same time, it cuts through any sense of nesting in feeling good and healthy. We feel sharp, tentative, precise, and spacious. Inquisitive mind is freed from the burden of ego-clinging, and we can actually see all the possibilities in a situation.

At first when insight arises, we do not know how to handle that experience, except by labeling it "thinking." But at the same time we feel the urge to go further. Going further does not mean abandoning the discipline of mindfulness. The simplicity of mindfulness is like an anchor: it connects us with the direct and precise experience of our basic wholesomeness and goodness. Going further means going beyond the idea that everything must have a purpose, including our practice. When we experience that our practice has no purpose, our awareness and sensitivity to the environment become acute. We begin to realize that awareness is present in the environment itself; therefore it needs no purpose. It is not *our* awareness; it does not depend on the reference point of ego at all.

At this point, awareness is seen as intelligent, self-existing, and continuous. This realization is based on true insight, that is, the direct knowledge of things as they are. That knowledge is not limited to a mere description or an accumulation of data. When inquisitive mind is liberated from the bonds of ego, we see the egoless nature of ourself and phenomena; therefore we realize that we do not have to struggle to survive. We do not need to speed or rush in order to accomplish a good and wholesome life.

NINE

STEPPING THROUGH
AN OPEN DOORWAY

IN ORDER TO PRACTICE VIPASHYANA properly, we should understand the attitude of accommodation. Accommodation refers to our ability to hear the dharma. If we are motivated by what we think we can get out of our practice and study of the dharma, then we cannot actually hear the teachings, nor can we take them to heart and practice them properly. In order to hear the teachings, it is necessary to remove the obstacle of personal goal orientation. Our state of mind must be free from aggression. The attitude of nonaggression, of not practicing for personal gain, is the accommodating attitude of vipashyana.

The basis of vipashyana is the experience of shamatha, which is marked by simplicity, precision, and accuracy. The practice of awareness naturally unfolds from the discipline of mindfulness. In fact, the two are inseparable in the sense that the experience of one leads to the experience of the other. So the practice of sitting meditation is still the basic discipline that develops awareness.

It is possible, however, that our mindfulness practice may become too tight, too goal-oriented, or too directional. When that happens, we need to develop a further sense of accommodation, of loosening up and feeling comfortable. When our strict approach to discipline opens up, a transition is taking place in our practice. We awaken to the environment around us, and we begin to feel space more than technique. This does not mean that technique is no longer necessary; it means that we no longer have to prove to ourselves that we are doing it. Relating to the literalness of the technique provides precision; but only when we relax and relate to the expansiveness of the environment does our centralized notion of a self start to dissolve.

When we are sitting, practicing the breathing technique, and labeling thoughts, we experience lapses in our practice characterized by drowsiness, agitation, or laziness. We become captivated by our thoughts, memories, fantasies, and so on, to the point that we become lost in our mental world. Suddenly, we experience a flash. In that flash of awareness there is no ego, no watcher.

We can make use of the flash of awareness in this way: when we become aware that we are not practicing the technique, we can allow ourselves to come back to the breath with a sense of accommodation and naturalness, without feeling good or bad, without struggling to get back. Generally, we say to ourselves, "I'm not doing the technique; I should be doing the technique." We feel tense and try to force ourselves to come back to the breath without effort. Usually we return to the breath when we remember that is what we are supposed to be doing. But as we progress in our practice, we begin to feel that coming back is not due to memory at all. The actual flash of awareness happens before we attach a description to it.

The experience of this flash of awareness brings the spontaneous awakening of prajna, discriminating awareness. Prajna is fully-liberated intelligence: it does not depend on the confirmation or feedback of ego. Therefore prajna is able to discriminate that which liberates us from that which binds us to confusion. Because it is egoless, prajna brings together intuitive experience and intellect, and allows us to completely identify with the teachings of the Buddha. It is prajna that enables us to

41

contemplate egolessness, impermanence, and suffering, and penetrate the teaching of the four noble truths.

The intellect of prajna is the discriminating aspect of mind, which ultimately leads to wisdom. Ordinarily, intellect is regarded as an analytical process that makes distinctions and puts things into categories. Intellect is usually associated with logic and some notion of proof: it provides confirmation for ego-centered experience. All this arises from the misconception that the function of intellect depends on a knower, a centralized basis of intelligence. However, intellect is fundamentally not dependent on ego. Neither does our intuitive perception need ego to function. Through vipashyana practice, both intellect and intuition are liberated from the bonds of ego.

Vipashyana frees us from grasping and ego-clinging. With the dawn of vipashyana we feel inspired to leave our confusion behind. It is like stepping through an open doorway, into a cool breeze of fresh air. For a long time, we have protected our confusion and hesitated to step through that doorway. But now we feel drawn to walk through, with full appreciation of what we are doing. This is the entrance to the *bodhisattva* path, to a wider vision and deeper commitment to practice. It is the birth of buddha mind, awakened mind.

PART II

Talking about this spark of wisdom is a very delicate matter and potentially explosive. Nevertheless, at some point it is necessary to proclaim our own quality of wakefulness, which is called buddha nature.

TEN

REMEMBERING WHO WE ARE

IN PRACTICING THE HINAYANA DISCIPLINE, we have been careful and precise, working hard to recover from the illness of confused ideas. All of that good discipline has prepared us to take one bold, strong step. That step is proclaiming that in each of us, there is a spark of wisdom that is absolutely uncontrollable. Talking about this spark of wisdom is a very delicate matter and potentially explosive. Nevertheless, at some point it is necessary to proclaim our own quality of wakefulness, which is called buddha nature.

As we practice meditation and develop mindfulness and awareness, there is a tendency to become insular, to create a subtle kind of fortification. As we file down the coarseness caused by passion, aggression, and ignorance, we begin to experience freedom from suffering. But our confidence is still in its infancy, and we fear we might regress to samsaric behavior. At that point, we might attempt to make our practice into a safeguard against the suffering of confusion. But not wanting to experience pain becomes a problem, because it is a gesture of defense rather than of liberation.

When we leave the environment of sitting practice and venture out, we encounter the world of confusion, which is harsh and unpredictable. The postmeditation experience is not quite as refined as we expected. We wonder whether we should take a chance on relating to all of it again. Will we lose our sense of peacefulness and clarity?

At some point we realize that our experience of mindfulness and awareness has no ground in itself. Because there is no confirmation of our existence, we feel naked. We find that Buddhism is not supporting us; there is no floor underneath at all. Then we become frightened and shocked. We realize that nothing, including our practice, can save us. We might even have second thoughts about our commitment to this path.

This is an extremely important point in our journey. We are about to make a transition into the mahayana, the great vehicle, the open way. This experience of vulnerability, which quivers and is not quite sure, is the stepping stone to the mahayana path. If we do not take that step, our practice could become solidified, like a monument that has no life of its own. Our practice has to expand to include the reality of postmeditation, which includes the reality of relationships. We realize that we can afford to be slightly more adventurous. We can afford to accommodate the noise, the din, the color, and the chaos.

Once we feel we have accomplished our discipline, we would like to protect it. The mahayana provides the means to protect it properly. The mahayana path is like the ultimate vaccine. This vaccine, which is made of illness itself, has to be reinjected into our system. This happens when we realize we cannot exclude the nonspiritual from our life. We cannot exclude the nonmindful and the nonaware. We have to accept negativity as part of our path.

In order to do that, we have to make friends with ourselves completely, by developing what is known as *maitri*, or loving kindness, kindness to ourselves. Kindness to ourselves means kindness to whatever negativity arises and to whatever seems to be outside our discipline. We have to learn to relax and readmit chaos, which means having an open heart. This open heart is like a wound: it is tender, throbbing and alive. It brings the delightful discovery that fundamentally we are really quite soft. But when we look around, we see the whole world is struggling with that vulnerability and tenderness, trying to build steel, concrete and glass over the soft earth. So the mahayana path begins with maitri, the kindness that waters the soft earth so the seed of buddha nature can grow.

The teachings of the mahayana proclaim that all beings possess an intrinsic and undeniable wakefulness, which is called buddha nature. In Sanskrit, it is known as *tathagatagarbha*, which means seed of the enlightened ones. *Tathagata* means enlightened one, and *garbha* means seed or womb. This fundamental, intrinsic wakefulness in us is both the starting point and the fulfillment of our human life. It is the cause of trying to achieve something and the achievement itself.

All of us would like to live a full and complete life and accomplish something meaningful. In that way we are different from the beings in other realms, such as animals, gods, or hungry ghosts, who do not share this uniquely human aspiration. Nevertheless, when we are born, we are born into confusion. Human existence is full of pain and discomfort, anxiety and expectation. Although our life is based on pure buddha nature, it is clouded by uncertainty.

The shock of birth makes us bewildered. Because we have no recollection of being born, we are constantly trying to remember who we are. We lose the clarity of intrinsic wakefulness, and we think, "Who am I?" Then we think, "If I am so and so, then how should I behave? How can I fulfill my life?" We are not sure, and because of that we try to create a way to be sure. We rely on the words of our parents, our peers and school teachers, our friends and relatives, our governments, and our books, in our attempt to remember who we are. We pursue diverse paths—spiritual, psychological, and material. But even our most wonderful thoughts and our greatest aspirations are linked to uncertainty about who we are.

Our efforts to remember can either breed further confusion or lead us to the genuine path. According to the mahayana teachings, tathagatagarbha is the seed of truly remembering who we are. It is the womb which gives birth to the tathagata, the fully awakened one. Tathagatagarbha is primordial goodness, that is, self-existing goodness without a reference point, good without contrast to bad. The potential to become buddha is already contained within us. When we realize our potential to become buddha, we start to recall our actual birth—not the physical birth of so and so, but our primordially good being. The clouds of uncertainty begin to disperse, and we discover a state of complete openness, which is vast and deep, free from concept, free from any reference point whatsoever.

The discovery of buddha nature leads to the development of compassion. Compassion is the natural expression of self-existing goodness. It is the basic instinct to care for others that exists in all beings. When we were born, someone nursed us so that our little body would survive. That was our mother. Without her, we would not be alive. Everyone has had someone who took care of him when he could not care for himself. Even the most vicious animals care for their young; the most hardened criminal has the capacity to love something or someone.

When we consider that fact, we cannot help but realize the basic tenderness and gentleness of our nature. We realize that we can be kind to ourselves, and furthermore we can radiate that kindness to others. The generation of compassion creates a river of kindness. That kindness continually benefits countless numbers of sentient beings and yet leaves no trace of its owner or bearer. In our lifetime, with great effort and true insight, we can give birth to compassion.

ELEVEN

THE PATH OF THE NOBLE ONES

THE MAHAYANA IS THE GREAT VEHICLE that can bring all sentient beings to the other shore, that is, deliver them from ignorance and suffering to enlightenment. But in order to enter this path, we should have a firm resolve to renounce samsara. We should realize that wandering in the confusion of samsara is a complete waste of time and is actually going against our buddha nature.

As we continue to practice, we become acutely aware of the suffering of others, realizing that all sentient beings are tortured by their own projections, believing them to be real. We see clearly that sentient beings are caught in the net of passion, aggression, and ignorance, in an immeasurable ocean of suffering. That ocean of samsara is so great and awful that we can never forget the sentient beings who are drowning in it. Therefore we make a commitment to practice diligently until samsara is completely emptied of confusion.

As we continue to practice, we realize that we cannot simply rely on our own feelings of accomplishment. For the first time we actually think beyond ourselves. We begin to take a genuine interest in everything around us. We realize we must do something that is not motivated merely by the desire for individual liberation.

Suddenly, almost unexpectedly, a wider space opens up. There is a feeling of something being born in us, expanding and waking up. That experience is the birth of *bodhicitta*. It is the experience of buddha nature becoming manifest. *Bodhi* means

51

awake; *citta* means heart, or mind. So bodhicitta means awaken-ed heart, or the mind of enlightenment.

Bodhi refers to the intrinsic wakefulness that is already in each of us. That wakefulness contains prajna, discriminating aware-ness. Because we are awake, we can see things clearly. When we see things clearly, we understand the nature of our own heart—the nature of *citta*—which is fundamentally decent, gentle and compassionate. Therefore we are not afraid to act from this wakefulness.

The activity of bodhicitta is traditionally divided into two categories: aspiration and practice. The aspiration of bodhicitta is the compassionate attitude that comes from our understand-ing of the suffering of sentient beings. It is our desire to attain enlightenment for the benefit of others. The practice of bodhi-citta is actually to carry out our aspiration by demonstrating our own wakefulness so that others, in turn, can realize they also possess immaculate bodhicitta.

Our aspiration to achieve enlightenment is transformed into practice only when we take the *bodhisattva* vow. A bodhisattva is a practitioner of the mahayana path. As we have said, *bodhi* means awake; *sattva* means being. So bodhisattva means awak-ened being. The bodhisattva vow, like the refuge vow, is a public statement, witnessed by the sangha and confirmed by the teacher. We vow that from now on we will be bodhisattvas: we will work and practice with complete wakefulness, so that other beings may follow that example. In doing so, we become part of the Buddha's family, the family of the awakened ones.

The bodhisattva's way has been called the path of the noble ones. Nobility is the heart of compassion. It is the true dignity of human birth, which is not based on the acquisition of wealth, power, or title in the ordinary sense. The bodhisattva's wealth is the heritage of buddha nature; the power to liberate others from suffering is bodhicitta; and the title, bodhisattva, acknowledges the pure dedication to achieving enlightenment.

Those who consider charity and good works to be the bodhisattva's path are missing the point. This path is not an ordinary one; in all the world there is no other like it. The noble family of the bodhisattvas is completely uncorrupted. The great lineage of bodhisattvas vowed to work ceaselessly for the sake of all sentient beings. They opened themselves and made the commitment to completely let go of personal territory. Ordinary practitioners would like to be content with their own practice and realization. But when we have the sincere desire to completely eliminate self-deception, undergo every hardship, and sacrifice our own comfort, then we can step forward firmly on this path.

When we take the bodhisattva vow, we acknowledge the workability of neurosis and confusion; otherwise we cannot be certain of overcoming the deceptions of ego. We have to give up any sense of personal security, of trying to protect our own territory, even if this includes our own practice and realization. We have to expose our neurosis and our embarrassment, our vulnerability, pride, dejection, and all the rest. We have to display these openly so that the warmth of compassion can dissolve any tendency to linger in samsara. Opening ourselves in this way is not a matter of becoming an exhibitionist, nor of looking for relief from pain. Neither are we trying to attract sympathy for ourselves. Giving up privacy is a way of overcoming fear and demonstrating that neurosis is workable in the context of discipline. This is the proper attitude of a bodhisattva.

By giving up privacy and forsaking any impulse to nest, hide, or protect ourselves from the turmoil of the world, we develop an enlightened attitude. The basis of an enlightened attitude is contained in the words of the bodhisattva vow, which say, "From now until I have become the very quintessence of enlightenment, I will develop an attitude directed towards unsurpassable, perfect, great enlightenment, so that the beings who have not yet crossed over may do so, who have not yet been delivered may be, who have not yet found relief may find it, and who have not yet passed into nirvana may do so." This means giving oneself completely to sentient beings.

Once we have taken the bodhisattva vow, we should go straight ahead. Shantideva, the great eighth-century mahayana teacher, writes in the *Bodhicaryavatara*, his treatise on "Entering the Practice of a Bodhisattva," that we have to become like a bridge that travelers walk over, like moonlight that cools the heat of passion, like medicine that cures disease, or like the sun, which illuminates the darkness of ignorance. As bodhisattvas we are willing to receive and embrace whatever occurs in our life. A sense of real vulnerability and openness is always present. We do not hesitate to expose ourselves to whatever pain, suffering, or chaos exists in the world.

It takes courage and a sense of peace and generosity to ourselves and others to actually embark upon this noble path. At the beginning, it does not matter that much whether our understanding is completely perfect. What is important is not holding back when people need us or when a situation needs our help. At the same time, we should not burst in when people don't want our help. We should have some feeling of pride and warriorship, but it is not necessary to crusade. There is no reason to attack or fight confusion. Being open and gentle brings tremendous confidence because it needs no defense. We can just be a vehicle for others to use to cross over the ocean of samsara and attain enlightenment.

TWELVE

THE SPIRITUAL FRIEND

MOTIVATED BY THE BODHISATTVA VOW, we embark on the open way of the mahayana path. We vow to make our sanity completely available to all sentient beings. As long as other people are suffering, we promise not to rest in an individual state of peace. But how can we accomplish the immense task of relating with everybody? The first step is to acknowledge our relationship with the teacher.

Most of us come into contact with the dharma because of our inquisitiveness and frustration. At the beginning of our journey, in the hinayana stage, we receive instruction from the teacher, who simply tells us how to be sane. The hinayana teacher is like a good physician who has the medicine that counteracts the poison of samsara. Because of our immediate need to hear the teachings and practice the path of sanity, our relationship with the teacher is at first somewhat distant. We are more interested in the teachings than in the personality of the teacher.

Practicing shamatha and vipashyana makes us feel healthier, but something still troubles us. We feel fine by ourselves, but we feel embarrassed with others. We might have discovered some sanity in ourselves, but when we relate with others it feels quite thin. In the midst of the chaos of relationships, our sanity seems fragile, and we wonder how to behave. After the illness of passion, aggression, and ignorance has been treated, a sense of emotion lingers. During our recovery period we feel slightly shaky, slightly unsure of our energy. Although we are on the way

55

to becoming well, it is still necessary to go back for a checkup. After our initial symptoms subside, we need to return to the teacher to make sure everything is completely cleared up.

We go back to the teacher, understanding that he actually saw us when we were sick. This is tremendously embarrassing. We had hoped our illness was completely cured, but in fact, we must see the teacher again. Although we know it is the best thing to do, we feel defensive. We think, "Why should I? I'm all right; there is no need for me to worry." It is so embarrassing that we wonder whether it is really necessary to have a personal teacher. But because of our embarrassment it is absolutely necessary. Our embarrassment is the fuel to actually work with all sentient beings and become a bodhisattva. With the help of the teacher, our embarrassment becomes the key that unlocks the treasury of the mahayana. Without our shaky quality, our clumsiness that makes our hands tremble and our mouth feel dry, without the fact that we don't know what to say, we could not work compassionately with all sentient beings. Only our personal relationship with the teacher shows us how to do that.

In the mahayana tradition, the teacher is known as the *kalyanamitra*, or spiritual friend. The physician of the hinayana becomes the friend in the mahayana. Relating with the spiritual friend is a very powerful experience. It involves our sense of being naked and vulnerable. At the same time there is some kind of magnetism or attraction. That is because the kalyanamitra embodies the qualities of the bodhisattva. We are too shy to acknowledge that, but we know it is true.

Meeting the spiritual friend is like meeting our lover for the first time. Having admired our lover from a distance, there comes a time when we have to say, "Hello." Perhaps the person will not respond, which might make us angry or depressed. But still, we anticipate that meeting and hope the person will become our intimate friend, our best friend.

The spiritual friend is actually the best friend we will ever have. He does not care whether we are the best or the worst. When we meet with our spiritual friend, it is very shocking: nothing happens; something happens; we cry; we laugh; we have lots of thoughts; or we feel blank. Sometimes we have many questions; at other times we don't have much to say. But no matter what happens, the spiritual friend always welcomes us wholeheartedly. He welcomes our delight, our irritation, our excitement, and our depression. The whole array of emotions that we display in front of the spiritual friend is heartily accepted.

Since the kalyanamitra has great compassion, he acts with spontaneous intelligence rather than out of convention. He has no hesitation about being human. He has unending warmth and openness and energy to work with us. He sees our buddha nature, and therefore he never regards our neurosis as something to be destroyed. Rather, he sees it as transparent, delightful, and workable. He is the only one who will encourage us to overcome all obstacles, no matter how difficult. Others might offer explanations, but the spiritual friend will say, "Go ahead."

The spiritual friend does not manifest as a divine being. He is one hundred percent human, and therefore he reflects our own human qualities. He actually eats and sleeps and goes to the bathroom. He is at once totally wise and totally humble. This throws us off guard and makes us even more embarrassed, because we see that we cannot hide anything. Working with the spiritual friend is so revealing, with all of its irritations and embarrassments, that we begin to understand what the bodhisattva path is all about. By not clinging to personal liberation and by opening ourselves to the spiritual friend, we begin to understand that our nakedness and embarrassment contain the seed of sanity. In other words, sanity is also present in our emotions. We realize we can expose our neurosis without being apologetic or arrogant. We feel as though we have rediscovered our own heart.

The spiritual friend is like a treasury that contains our inheritance as human beings. In fact, the kalyanamitra represents our emotional connection to all sentient beings. He is like a clear mirror that reflects whatever is put in front of it. Our relationship with the spiritual friend encompasses our entire emotional world. At different times he is like a husband or wife, a teacher, a friend, a lover, a yogin, a scholar, or a poet. We become quite infatuated and in awe of this person, to the point where we become inspired to emulate his dedication to all sentient beings. Through our relationship with the spiritual friend we see that enlightenment can be embodied in a human being; it need not remain a distant goal. Therefore the spiritual friend should be sought out, venerated, and requested to teach.

THIRTEEN

EMPTINESS

MAKING FRIENDS WITH OURSELVES and discovering the spacious world of the kalyanamitra, in which we can afford to be open, is very exciting. That feeling of actually waking up, discovering our buddha nature—realizing that our neurosis, our preoccupation with ourselves, is merely a temporary obstacle—is tremendously inspiring. However, this excitement could be misleading. It might blind us to the true nature of compassion.

True compassion is the result of experiencing *shunyata*. *Shunya* means empty; and *ta* means "ness." The doctrine of emptiness is the essential teaching of the mahayana. It is the ultimate truth of non-ego. In fact, it is beyond non-ego; it is no ego. Even to say that shunyata is an "it" is misleading. Nevertheless, it is necessary to speak in terms of shunyata experience in order to understand how to practice the mahayana teachings.

The experience of shunyata occurs as a glimpse of unconditioned mind. For a moment, there is no project whatsoever, no occupation, no dwelling in past, present, or future. There are no preconceptions and no alternatives. In a flash, there is no sense of hanging on to anything. Initially this experience is brought about by contrast. As beginning practitioners, we experience a vivid contrast between meditation and postmeditation. There is a definite shift at the end of a practice session, which we might regard as a relief. We feel as though we have let go of something, finished something. That feeling is deceptive because it comes from making a distinction between practice and everyday life.

We feel there are two worlds: the world of our practice, which has become familiar and trustworthy, and the world of postmeditation, which is still in question. Nevertheless, when we experience the contrast between those two, that brings a glimpse of shunyata.

The experience of shunyata does not happen because of any plan or scheme; it happens suddenly, spontaneously. We cannot even say, "I just experienced shunyata," because there is no memory of "I" in the experience. At the same time, the experience of shunyata is not a state of blankness. It is a state of total awareness, devoid of self-consciousness. That experience is primordial; it is not the accumulation of preconceived ideas.

Those who recognize shunyata are those who practice, because the practice itself is designed so that we can recognize it. As we take part in the environment of discipline, we also create our own version of what we are doing. In the midst of trying to maintain that, we experience a gap. That moment is empty of all preconceptions. At that point there is no beginning, no middle, and no end. There is just what is, which is shunyata.

Experientially, shunyata can be described in terms of vastness and profundity. Profundity is the discovery that all beings, and in fact all phenomena are from beginningless time without ego. Vastness is total relaxation and freedom from clinging to existence. When we experience both profundity and vastness together, we give birth to compassion. Compassion arises as the genuine expression of sympathy and friendliness to all sentient beings who suffer in samsara because they have not realized the egoless nature of existence. Compassion radiates the warmth of primordial goodness in all directions. That warmth has no limit because it has its origin in shunyata. The mind of true compassion is this: there is no doer, there is no act of doing, and there is no recipient of the action. Because of that, we can communicate with others unobstructedly.

FOURTEEN

TAKING OUR PLACE IN THE WORLD

THE STARTING POINT OF THE MAHAYANA path is the affirmation of the existence in all beings of buddha nature, primordial goodness. Through the practices of shamatha and vipashyana, buddha nature is awakened, and that sparks the first glimpse of compassion in ourselves. Even though neurosis pops up, that spark of wakefulness continues to grow. Relating with ourselves becomes less heavy-handed, more workable, and more manageable. As we realize we can handle ourselves quite easily, a sense of strength and confidence develops. That feeling of workability is maitri: gentleness and kindness to ourselves. When we experience true maitri, we realize we can extend that gentleness and kindness into our world by committing ourselves to the path of wakefulness, the mahayana. In doing so we begin to arouse the bodhicitta in our heart. From that, we give birth to the notion that we can achieve enlightenment for the sake of all sentient beings.

Bodhicitta, the essence of kindness, is further awakened by taking the bodhisattva vow, which proclaims that from this day onward, "I will devote all of my energy, practice, body, speech, and mind to the benefit of others. I will attain enlightenment, not for my own benefit, but for the benefit of others." In order to carry out this vow, we must become generous. This means that we no longer regard practicing meditation and relating with others as separate events. Rather, our practice of meditation unfolds in such a way that relating with others becomes meditation in action. Having seen the egolessness of self and the egolessness of all beings, we are freed from the burden of self-interest. Bodhicitta matures, and the spark of compassion becomes a flame, radiating warmth in all directions. Joy arises spontaneously and naturally, and working for the benefit of others is no longer a chore.

The spiritual friend is of primary importance in developing this sense of delight. Without such a friend, who has practiced and achieved liberation, it would be impossible to clear away the veils of ignorance and conflicting emotions. The spiritual friend creates an atmosphere free from conditions. In that space we can expose our fear, doubt, pride, and our sense of accomplishment; there is no reason to hold back and try to maintain our territory or security. When we work with the spiritual friend, we encounter the vast space of compassionate mind, in which it is possible to completely let go. Usually letting go means not caring what happens; but in this case, letting go means surrendering to greater openness. Although we may sometimes feel threatened or shy or inadequate, because of the generosity of the spiritual friend, we realize that those feelings are actually the fuel for the attainment of enlightenment.

In order to realize the mahayana path, we have to perfect what are known as the transcendent actions of the bodhisattva, the *six paramitas. Param* means "other shore" and *ita* means "gone"; so paramita means to reach the farthest shore—to transcend, attain perfection. The six paramitas are: generosity, discipline, patience, exertion, meditation, and knowledge or prajna. These actions are called transcendent because they are not defiled by ego and can therefore cut through the chain of cause and effect. They are also called virtuous actions, not in the sense of personal adornment but as ultimate virtues that go beyond conventional ideas of good and bad.

When we begin to practice the paramitas, there is a sense of self-conscious effort. As we continue, these practices become the spontaneous realization and demonstration of our bodhisattva vow. The essence of paramita practice is taking on the suffering of others without giving back anything harmful. All suffering is taken on ourselves; all good is given to others. This practice is impossible without the experience of egolessness. As long as we cling to existence, there is no way to take on the pain of others and, in fact, all we can do is perpetuate suffering. By being empty and transparent, by not holding on to the notion of ego, we can actually change the world.

The bodhisattva activity of the paramitas arises spontaneously from meditation practice. We realize that if we lack generosity, it is because we are hoarding our wealth as a means of security; if we are not disciplined, it is because we have no respect for others; if we are not patient, it is because we have not tamed aggression; if we are not energetic, then there is no inspiration for others; and if we do not meditate, then our mind bounces back and forth between clarity and cloudiness. Finally, we realize that if we do not develop prajna, then the knowledge of how to be of supreme benefit to others eludes us. Prajna is that which sees shunyata. With the clear vision of prajna, we recognize buddha nature in all beings, and we act without self-interest. Having accomplished the paramitas, we take our place in the world as a bodhisattva who has a true and noble heart filled with compassion.

The result of practicing the paramitas is the realization of greater vision. That vision sees that, from the very beginning, all beings possess primordial wisdom, the wisdom of letting go. This kind of wisdom is called *jnana* in Sanskrit and *yeshe* in Tibetan. Jnana is wisdom that is primordially pure and self-existing. It is totally available all the time. Jnana is vast space, which is the openness of mind, accompanied by unceasing energy. It is the union of shunyata and compassion. When space and energy are realized as indivisible, then wisdom dawns in the form of *mahakaruna,* great compassion: all actions become beneficial because they are not motivated by hope and fear. The dharma is seen as completely pure and continually existing. The world as it is becomes the self-existing realm of the buddhas.

PART III

All in all, the desire for enlightenment, for fulfillment, for realization, abides in the image of the guru.

FIFTEEN

TOTAL ENVIRONMENT

IT WOULD BE BENEFICIAL TO DISCUSS the prospect of hearing the vajrayana teachings. *Vajra* is a Sanskrit word that means indestructible, diamondlike; and *yana,* as before, means vehicle. So the vajrayana is the indestructible vehicle, the complete teachings of the Buddha. This vehicle encompasses both the hinayana and mahayana disciplines in the sense that the vajrayana is the fruition of the two previous yanas. The hinayana and mahayana create a firm foundation that enables the practitioner to be brought to the point of spontaneous awakening.

The heart of the vajrayana teachings is the realization that the phenomenal world and one's mind form an indestructible unity, which includes the defilements of ego as well as the purity of practice. Thus at this stage of the path, every element of existence is seen as sacred; nothing is rejected. In the previous yanas, there is a notion of direction. That is to say, in the hinayana and mahayana we start from confused existence and proceed on the path of dharma in order to uncover awakened mind. But in the vajrayana, we begin with the proclamation of *vajra nature,* the indestructible and primordially pure nature of all beings. Because all beings possess vajra nature, enlightenment is no longer viewed as a conclusion, but as the starting point of practice. Practice is not seen as a means to an end, but as the expression of awakened mind in everyday life.

These teachings are sometimes called the secret teachings: because of their directness and simplicity, they can easily be missed. They are also known as secret because it can be extremely dangerous to proclaim vajra nature as the starting point. The danger here is that without the proper training, students might confuse neurosis with enlightenment. Without thoroughly exhausting ego by means of the disciplines of mindfulness, awareness, renunciation, and dedicating one's life to others, receiving the vajrayana teachings would be destructive.

At this point in our journey, our experience of practice should be continuous rather than marked by highs and lows. However, there still might be some sense of holding back. There might be some little corner, some little pocket we would like to reserve for ourselves. It is not necessary to analyze what that reservation might be. But in order to become a student of the vajrayana, we cannot carry with us any hidden reservations. If we try to do so, the vajrayana will remain secret, because it demands total commitment, total hearing, total contemplation, and total meditation.

When we enter the vajrayana, we must pay complete attention to what is being said. We must take part in the total environment of the path we are about to enter. When we take that step, expectations or wishful thinking will not help us; only aspiration based on a solid foundation of discipline, only total awareness, will help. So we must join the vajra atmosphere and commit ourselves to the totality of the vajrayana teachings.

Suppose we aspire to accomplish a particular goal in our life—let's say, to become a bank teller. We work very hard to get an interview with the personnel director of the bank; we want the job badly. We would like to be accepted as a teller among tellers. So we straighten up and put on our best suit of clothes. We try to be correct and dignified so that we will be hired. We feel we have the intelligence to be a bank teller, but we must impress the manager with our ability to do it, and that involves how we present ourselves.

In the same way, when we enter the vajrayana, how we present ourselves is extremely important. Obviously, we cannot present a facade, because without the proper qualifications, we will surely not be accepted. Neither can we be naive in our wish to be accepted. There is something more than that. It is absolutely necessary that our motivation and intention be perfectly pure.

To become a student of the vajrayana, we must realize egolessness of self and other. We must have generated the heart of tenderness, bodhicitta, so as not to cling to egolessness as a mode of being. And furthermore, we must have unshakable conviction in the truth of the teachings. But first and foremost, as students of the vajrayana, we must have a clear perception of our teacher as the embodiment of enlightenment. We must realize that the vajrayana teachings are inseparable from the vajra master.

In the hinayana, the student experiences the teacher as wise and fatherly; in the mahayana, as an intimate friend who cares for the student's well-being. In the vajrayana, the teacher is called the vajra master, or *vajracarya*. Only the vajra master understands that the power of the vajrayana teachings is so great that, without proper preparation, the presentation of naked truth could undermine a student't progress, rather than provoking spontaneous realization. So in order to practice the vajrayana teachings, it is absolutely necessary to have a qualified and authentic vajra master or guru.

In entering the vajrayana, how should we regard the guru, the one who presents the teachings? The guru himself is the living buddha; he is none other than buddha. He is the supreme example of sanity. Passion, aggression, and ignorance do not come into play with him. No matter whom he encounters in his life, he is not biased. He is absolutely not moved by the winds of conflicting emotions. His body, speech, and mind are completely synchronized. Whatever he says, whatever he does, is completely pure and straightforward, without deception. He is elegant, and he serves to enrich the world and all sentient beings. He has perfected the stages of the path and thoroughly realized vajra nature. He is completely accomplished, and therefore he can deliver buddha into the palm of your hand.

It has been said that even the enlightened ones of previous times paid homage to the vajra masters who imparted the teachings of vajrayana to them. And if they have done so, what about ourselves? Seeing our guru as buddha is essential to receiving these teachings. We might have conflicting thoughts about our guru, but those thoughts are inconsequential. The truth is that the one who presents the complete teaching to us can be none other than buddha. When we regard our guru in that way, our mind opens and we receive the teachings without hesitation.

SIXTEEN

ENTERING THE GURU'S WORLD

ONCE WE HAVE COMMITTED OURSELVES to the guru, how do we approach him in order to receive the vajrayana teaching? We join our hands together: that is the gesture of supplicating the guru, the one who presents the ultimate teaching. We join our hands together at the level of our heart, and we bow our head. That gesture is one of immense gratitude for having the good fortune to hear these teachings in our lifetime. That is the appropriate way to approach the guru of the vajrayana.

In doing so, we are not trying to manipulate or court the vajra master. We are affirming the respect we have for our own intelligence as well as for the guru. We are closing the gap, so to speak; we are closing the gap between doubt and speculation by pressing our hands together at the level of our heart. At the same time we are overcoming the frivolity of our habitual way of making a request and our awkwardness in approaching the teacher. That display is the recognition that the presence of the guru cuts frivolity, laziness, and doubt on the spot. Therefore joining our hands and bowing our head slightly is not simply a physical gesture; it is a portrait of our state of mind.

At that point, how should we conduct ourselves? We should make a prostration; we should surrender body, speech, and mind to the one who transmits the teachings to us. We have committed ourselves to the environment of the teachings, and we have approached the guru properly. Now, we prostrate, which means, "No matter what obstacle occurs, I will give my

71

total being to this path, to this practice." When we prostrate, we are declaring that we will not hold on to any comfort whatsoever. We are prostrating and giving up clinging to the past. There is no need to hold back, because there is no fear of the repercussions. That is making prostration: surrendering body, speech, and mind to the guru.

When we prostrate to the vajra master, that alone does not completely make us fit to receive teaching. We must also make some offering. What is it that we offer? We should offer the very best expression of our desire for enlightenment.

Marpa was the father of the Kagyü lineage in Tibet. He lived in the eleventh century. When he wanted to return to India for what was to be his final visit to his vajra master, the great Indian pandit Naropa, he gathered a great sum of gold dust, because that was considered the very best offering. He worked very strenuously to accumulate that gold, and then he brought it to India and offered it to his guru, Naropa. After many months of hardship and searching for Naropa, he presented the gold dust, saying, "Please give me the teachings." Marpa offered the gold dust, but Naropa said, "You should offer this to the three jewels," and he threw it into the jungle. Then he said to Marpa, who was dumbfounded, "If you desire gold, look at this." Naropa opened his hands, and they were filled with gold dust. Then he struck the ground with his foot, and the entire surroundings became gold. And then some realization arose in Marpa.

Marpa was not in the least stingy. He worked very hard and offered all that he had in order to receive the teachings. Our mentality towards receiving the vajrayana teachings should be the same as his. Any wealth, fame, good fortune—anything in our life that is good and wholesome—we should actually offer in order to receive the vajrayana teaching. When we offer, there might be some sense of, "Look what a great thing I'm giving you. I am surrendering my body, speech, and mind. Isn't it wonderful that I can give you something?" But when we offer something, we should offer it completely. This is symbolic of not holding on to any spiritual insurance policy. In other words, we should not wait for a response to our offering. We should realize on the spot that these teachings are so precious and so real that they cannot be bargained for at all. If we do not understand this, we can never completely enter the world of the vajra master.

Milarepa was the foremost student of Marpa. When he went to meet Marpa, he wanted the teachings very badly; however, Milarepa did not have any gold. When Marpa asked him, "What is your offering?" Milarepa replied, "All I have to offer is my body, speech, and mind." Then Marpa said that whether or not Milarepa would attain enlightenment in his lifetime would depend solely on his effort. That is the kind of offering we must make. We must offer our intention to manifest as a fully awakened being. We must offer our effort and, with that effort, we must build a palace of enlightenment. That is the vajrayana approach.

After offering, we feel some sense of having connected to the vajra world, the guru's world. Having entered the guru's world, the next step is to follow his instructions. Because the guru sees that our basic intention is without passion, aggression, or ignorance, he is extremely pleased. We have come to him with folded hands, prostrated, and made our offering. We have offered our purest intention to achieve the essence of buddhadharma, the enlightenment of all the buddhas. He is delighted to teach us, and now we must follow his instructions. Following the guru's instructions is not just a matter of listening to his words. It means committing ourselves to the total, sacred world that he presents. Following the guru's instructions is the ultimate offering. As Milarepa said, "All I can do is follow your example."

SEVENTEEN

THE MEANING OF DEVOTION

[The following four chapters are a commentary on "The Story of Red Rock Agate Valley," the first song in the famed *Hundred Thousand Songs of Milarepa*. A translation of this song, prepared by the Nalanda Translation Committee, under the direction of Vajracarya the Venerable Chögyam Trungpa, Rinpoche is appended here divided into four parts. The relevant sections appear at the beginning of the appropriate chapters.   —ED.]

THE STORY OF RED ROCK AGATE VALLEY

NAMO GURAVE[1]

Once the Lord of yogins,[2] Jetsün[3] Milarepa, was dwelling in the state of luminous mahamudra[4] at the Fortress of Garudas[5] in Agate Valley. At one point, he arose to prepare a meal. He couldn't find any wood in the firepit, much less any flour, salt, or thickener. Also, there was no water and no embers in the stove. Mila thought, "I have let these things go too long. I should go and gather some wood."

When he had gathered enough wood in the folds of his robe, a great wind suddenly arose. When Mila held on to his robe, the wood blew away. When he clutched the wood, his robe blew away. He thought, "Although I have stayed such a long time in retreat, I still have not let go of attachment. What is the use of practicing the dharma if I don't let go of attachment?" And he said, "If the wind blows my robe away, let it. If it blows the wood away, let it." He let go of them both and stood there.

However, due to his lack of nourishment, with the next gust of wind Mila fell down in a faint for a while.

When he awoke, the wind had calmed and his robe was dangling from the top of a tree. He felt sad and sat in meditation atop a boulder the size of a sheep.

THE KAGYÜ LINEAGE IS CALLED the oral-instruction lineage. *Ka* means word or command, and *gyü* means lineage or continuity. So *Kagyü* means the continuity or lineage of the guru's command—in other words, the continuity of oral instruction. The oral instructions of this lineage have continued in unbroken succession from the time of Tilopa to the present day. Tilopa, who lived in India in the tenth century, was the forefather of the Kagyü lineage. He received teachings from four gurus, and in addition he received the vajrayana teachings through his direct realization of the awakened state. Tilopa passed his teachings on to Naropa; Naropa gave transmission to Marpa; and Marpa transmitted his wisdom to the great yogin, Milarepa.

Altogether, the Kagyü lineage is based on the transmission of the awakened state of mind from guru to student. That transmission only occurs in the atmosphere of devotion. Devotion to the teacher arises when we have had some glimpse of enlightenment. That glimpse creates open space, and in that open space is the possibility of clear communication. When that openness is accompanied by heartfelt longing for the teacher, the embodiment of the awakened state, a meeting of minds between the guru and the student is possible.

When the guru and the student experience a meeting of minds, that creates a mutual bond, a mutual commitment to complete enlightenment. On that basis of mutual trust, the guru can transmit the vajrayana teachings to the student. Transmission takes place when the guru points out the nature of reality, that is, the enlightened quality of one's mind. Such transmission

78

can occur in three ways. It can occur by meeting the guru's mind directly, that is, transmission beyond thought. Or it can occur through gesture or symbol, which points out enlightened mind in the phenomenal world. Finally, transmission can occur through oral instruction. But without devotion, transmission is impossible.

Devotion is not a matter of blind faith, fanaticism, or sentimentality. Genuine devotion is full of precision and clarity, and rests on the perfection of mindfulness and awareness. With devotion we can hear the guru's instructions clearly and follow them precisely. Without devotion, we might receive instructions, but it would be impossible to understand them or put them into practice. Devotion cuts through our mental fog of doubt and speculation, and therefore, we are able to practice the instructions of the guru on the spot, without hesitation. The result of taking to heart the instructions of the guru and following them completely is the attainment of enlightenment.

The great yogin, Milarepa is the foremost example of how a human being like ourselves practiced devotion to his guru and attained enlightenment. When Milarepa was still a youth, his father died. Milarepa's uncle and aunt usurped his father's estate and made servants of him and his family. Milarepa's mother, angry over losing the family fortune and lands, sent him to study black magic. She wanted her son to avenge the injustice and humiliation they had suffered. Milarepa was so devoted to his mother that he did what she asked. He studied hard and perfected the art of sorcery. Then, using the magic he had acquired, he brought down destruction and chaos on his aunt and uncle and everyone else who had taken part in the downfall of his family.

Because of his devotion to his mother and his longing to relieve her suffering, Milarepa was able to direct his mind one-pointedly, and he accomplished what he set out to do. However, his devotion was misguided. In his fervor, he failed to realize that his actions would cause even more suffering. Likewise, if we think that attaining enlightenment will bring us power over others, we are mistaken; and if our intentions are mistaken, then our ability to follow spiritual instructions and achieve power or clarity or precision will only cause more chaos. Therefore, in developing an attitude of devotion, we must have a firm understanding of the law of karma, cause and effect.

When Milarepa eventually met his guru, Marpa, he had to labor many years and undergo severe trials and hardships. Why? So that he could relate to his past actions, the karma he created, and acknowledge that he had actually caused harm. Whether or not he was naive at the time, Milarepa did commit those particular crimes. When one causes destruction, harm, or chaos to others, that is a crime. It was Marpa's duty to point that out to Milarepa by whatever means possible, so that Milarepa could overcome his own negative karma. It is the same with us. Practicing meditation is not a matter of abandoning pain or erasing our memory of it. In fact, by practicing, our experience of suffering becomes more vivid. If we do not acknowledge having caused harm to ourselves and others, there is no way to go further. We cannot receive the precious instructions that lead to liberation, without taking responsibility for our whole life.

When we meet a genuine guru, we develop a deep longing to practice and attain that state of wholesomeness which is the complete fulfillment of our life as a human being. Milarepa saw in his guru the quality of the awakened state of mind, and he knew that was what he wanted to achieve. Our experience is precisely the same. In recognizing the awakened state of mind of the guru, we long to follow his example.

After studying with Marpa and following his instructions for many years, Milarepa received transmission and went to practice in solitude. He practiced diligently for a long time. Because he was so keen on achieving enlightenment, he neglected ordinary things; he even neglected taking care of his own body. Milarepa's meditative absorption became so great that he ate very little food and hardly gave thought to replenishing his supplies. When he finally realized that he needed to eat, if only to continue practicing, he left his meditation retreat in search of provisions. Suddenly a storm arose, and the wind tore at his robes. When Milarepa tried to hold on to the firewood he had collected, his clothing blew away, and when he tried to hold on to his clothing, the firewood blew away.

When we practice, we realize some sanity in ourselves. But if we try to hold on to it, it slips away. On the other hand, if we deliberately try to let go, we become distracted. If we try to contain the experience of meditation, we find it is like a wet bar of soap constantly slipping out of our hand. Milarepa realized that mind is not something that can be captured or contained. The analogy of the wind, the firewood, and Milarepa's clothing points out that until we abandon clinging, our experience will not be stable.

After practicing for a time, we might feel that we have accomplished something. However, as soon as we get up from our meditation cushion, we forget our practice. We become so fascinated by phenomena that we completely lose our perspective. We become as engrossed in making a cup of tea as Milarepa was in trying to gather firewood. We see a teacup looming in front of us like a jewel. As we reach for it, we suddenly wonder, "Why am I getting so excited about this?" Then we wonder whether our practice is having any effect. We think, "This really isn't getting me anywhere. I feel like giving it up."

81

Eventually we become disappointed in our practice and in the teachings. When our experience does not meet our expectations, we become disillusioned and think about giving up. We think, "I'll never be free of attachment to this ego. The whole thing seems completely hopeless; I might as well forget it." As Milarepa said, "What is the use of practicing the dharma if I don't let go of attachment?" After practicing for so long, he still felt he was clinging to ego. We practice for so long and it seems to be so simple and good. Then just a little thought, like having a cup of tea, completely steals our awareness.

In Milarepa's experience, his cup of tea was the firewood and his practice was his clothing. He wanted to maintain his practice, but at the same time he wanted that firewood. That is what we do. We want to hold on to our practice, but we think we need a cup of tea. They both appear to be completely real and vivid and necessary, and we don't see how we can let go of either one. So we are blown back and forth by our confusion. Finally, everything is so frustrating that continuing seems pointless.

Milarepa studied with his guru for some time, but then he had to practice alone. At that point all he had was the instructions of his teacher. He followed them as best as he could, and when his discipline and devotion broke down he tried to repair them. But he felt he could not go on, so he gave up. Then Milarepa said, "If the wind blows my robe away, let it. If it blows the wood away, let it," and he fainted away from weakness. When he came to, he saw his robe hanging from the branch of a tree. He understood at once the impermanence and fickleness of this world. He saw that the reality of the world was like that bit of cloth. A tremendous feeling of renunciation arose in him. He sat up, and on that very spot began to meditate.

If we are fortunate, we wake up and see the complete chaos and futility of our world. At that moment, we understand why our guru told us to practice. That is when devotion increases and renunciation is affirmed. Giving up fascination with our own survival, we see that all of our experience is like Milarepa's robe hanging from the tree. That overwhelming realization brings us back to practice.

To begin with we have devotion to our guru, and therefore we follow his instructions. As we practice, we realize that devotion includes paying attention to every detail of our life. Every moment we forget, faint a little bit, and come back. Let us take our own frustration as an opportunity to wake up. The shock of waking up reveals the futility of samsara and the true meaning of devotion.

EIGHTEEN

LONGING

Then, to the East, in the direction of Trowo valley, a white cloud was floating. Mila thought, "Under that cloud over there is the dharma place of Trowo valley. There dwells my guru, the translator Marpa Lotsawa."

Mila remembered the father guru expounding the tantras,[6] giving abhishekas,[7] and oral instructions in the midst of his wife and a gathering of vajra brothers and sisters and attendants. He thought, "If Marpa were there now, I would go to see him no matter what happened."

On top of his earlier sadness, Mila felt immeasurably intense sadness in remembering the guru. He shed many tears and sang this song of sad longing, "The Six Remembrances of the Guru."

Venerable Marpa, merely remembering you, father, dispels
    longing.
Lord Marpa, this lowly one sings a song of longing.

To the East of the Red Rock Agate Valley
A white cloud floats.
Under this floating misty white cloud
Is a back range of mountains like a posed elephant.
The range in front is like a great posed lion.
On that mountain, at the holy place, the dharma place of
    Trowo valley,
On a great throne of marble,
On a seat of antelope skin—

Who else could sit there
But Marpa the Translator.
What joy if you were there now!
Though my devotion is meager, how I long to see you!
Though my longing is meager, how I long to see you!
The more I contemplate, the more I remember the authentic
  guru.
The more I meditate, the more I remember Marpa Lotsawa.

Your wife Dagmema, who is better than any mother—
What joy if she were there now!
Though the journey is long, how I long to see her!
Though the path is difficult to travel, how I long to see her!
The more I contemplate, the more I remember the authentic
  guru.
The more I meditate, the more I remember Marpa Lotsawa.

The profound *Hevajra Tantra*[8]—
What joy if it were being taught now!
Though my understanding is meager, how I long to learn it!
Though my intellect is meager, how I long to study it!
The more I contemplate, the more I remember the authentic
  guru.
The more I meditate, the more I remember Marpa Lotsawa.

The four sign abhishekas of the hearing lineage[9]—
What joy if they were being performed now!
Though my offering is small, how I long to request it!
Though I lack the abhisheka offering, how I long to request it!
The more I contemplate, the more I remember the authentic
  guru.
The more I meditate, the more I remember Marpa Lotsawa.

The profound instructions of the six yogas of Naropa[10]—
What joy if they were being taught now!

Though my perseverance is meager, how I long to request
   them!
Though my exertion in practice is meager, how I long to
   practice them!
The more I contemplate, the more I remember the authentic
   guru.
The more I meditate, the more I remember Marpa Lotsawa.

The faithful assembly of dharma friends of Ü and Tsang—
What joy if they were there now!
Though my experience and realization are weak, how I long
   to compare with them!
Though my understanding is inferior, how I long to compare
   this with them!
The more I contemplate, the more I remember the authentic
   guru.
The more I meditate, the more I remember Marpa Lotsawa.

Though in the state of devotion, this lowly one is inseparable
   from you.
Remembering the guru with wholehearted longing
I am tormented by desire and overwhelmed.
I am so choked up I cannot speak.
Kind one, please dispel this son's longing.
Thus Mila sang.

DEVOTION IS OFTEN MISUNDERSTOOD. Our ideas of devotion are
often clouded by misconceptions or wishful thinking. We think
there is someone who could absorb our ignorance and irritation,
someone greater than we are, who could act as a kind of cosmic
sponge. On the other hand, we feel that relying on someone else
is a kind of slavery or giving up of individuality. We wonder why
we should be devoted to anyone at all. If our meditation practice
seems to be going well, what need is there for devotion? Real

devotion does not come from discursive thoughts about whom we should be devoted to or why. Real devotion springs from disgust with samsara, nausea with endless, needless suffering and pain.

If we can actually see how useless and unnecessary it is to remain ignorant and confused, then devotion begins to beat in our heart. Until there is real aversion to samsara, we cannot give birth to genuine devotion. Holding on to expectations, thoughts, or experiences of the past, present, or future is utterly meaningless: "Even though my past experiences have been disappointing, maybe in the future, things will be better." If we cling to fascination for what we might get, then there is no room for devotion to grow in us. When we see that samsara is nothing but a rotting corpse, we come to a turning point in our journey.

The guru is the key element in this transition. His very existence provides a vivid contrast to the insanity of samsara. It is obvious that the guru has no allegiance to confusion. At the same time, he demonstrates the brilliance of a fully enlightened human being. He is the treasury, the repository of the teachings. Because of his example, our devotion becomes the confidence to overcome obstacles on the path.

In Milarepa's song, we read how he regained his composure and resumed meditating. At that point, Milarepa was overcome by tremendous longing for his guru. He thought "If I could just be with my guru." As we endeavor to accomplish our practice, our mindfulness and awareness come and go. That becomes a reminder of the futility of lingering in samsara. Then the thought of the guru arises and sparks us to persevere in our practice.

Remembering the guru brings a vivid sense of nowness, and we long to throw off the dullness of ignorance. The thought of the guru arises in our mind like the thought of home. Although we may be far from home, it still seems so real to us. We feel as though we can smell the flowers in the garden and see the pattern on the bedroom wallpaper. We can even hear the voices of our family. Even if the time we spent with the guru was brief, when we think of him, we feel so lonely. Seeing his picture or even hearing about him evokes a recollection of that time when we felt completely at home with ourselves. We remember the kindness of the one who taught us the dharma, and we recall those moments when we felt completely unfettered, just listening to the guru's words.

Eventually we have to go off on our own, just as Milarepa did. We have to relate with the world around us—our family, our home, our job, our car, and so on. We try to practice and study the teachings, and at the same time take care of the necessities of life. In the midst of all that, we are overcome by a feeling of sadness. "If I could only be with my guru, listening to him teach. It was so simple and fresh. Now everything seems so desolate and lonely." We think of the guru, the Buddha, Tilopa, Marpa, and Milarepa—all the great lineage holders of the past—and we are deeply touched. They practiced so diligently, even though it was lonely. They worked so hard to be able to pass down these precious teachings to us.

Contemplating in this way, we come to a crossroads where loneliness becomes aloneness. In the midst of complaining about ourselves and our problems, we suddenly feel totally alone, as Milarepa did. What we yearn for seems so distant and far away, and we long to be one with it. At the same time, because of our practice, it seems to be right here, in the very moment, and we can almost touch it.

Milarepa said, "The more I meditate, the more I remember my guru." Because the separation from the guru is so real, tangible, and vivid, we contemplate his teachings over and over. The more we contemplate his teachings, the more we practice.

The more we practice, the more we recognize the guru as the embodiment of the awakened state, and the more we long to realize that ourselves. That longing is like a rip or tear in our heart. The more our heart is torn apart, the more we think of the guru and the dharma.

When we feel that sense of separation—"I haven't quite got it yet; I haven't understood"—then the image of the guru arises. All in all, the desire for enlightenment, for fulfillment, for realization, abides in the image of the guru. Even when we see a painting or a statue of the Buddha, longing for the awakened state of mind is kindled in us. We cannot manufacture this longing; we have to experience it. That can happen only when we encounter someone who presents the truth without apology. Longing for the guru is the same as longing for the extinction of ego. Such longing produces great practice.

NINETEEN

GRATITUDE

The cloud stretched out like five rolls of silk of different colors. On top of it, Lord Marpa himself arrived, his dignity even greater than before, riding a white lioness adorned with many ornaments.

Marpa said, "Son, great magician, what has happened now that you should call out to me with such fervent longing? Have you lost faith in the guru, yidam,[11] and three jewels? Have you been following negative discursive thoughts? Have the obstacles of the eight worldly dharmas[12] entered your house of practice? Have the demons of hope and fear bothered and irritated you?

"Offer up service to the guru and the three jewels. Give gifts down to sentient beings of the six realms. Between the two, haven't the favorable circumstances of purifying your evil deeds and obscurations and cultivating virtues arisen in you? No matter what, we cannot be separated. Therefore, practice and accomplish benefit for the teachings and sentient beings."

Hearing Marpa say this, Mila experienced unbearably intense joy, and within this state, he sang this song of his experience that arose in reply to Marpa's words.

I saw the face of the father guru and heard his words,
And the depression of this lowly one arose as meditative
    experience.
By remembering the example of the guru,
Realization was born in my depths.
The blessings of your kindness literally entered me.

All antidharmic thoughts ceased.
This song of longing in remembering you, guru,
Although it may irritate the ears of the jetsun,
This lowly one has no other thoughts but these.
I will continually arouse my devotion; please protect me with
    your kindness.

My practice of enduring suffering with perseverance
Is service that pleases the father guru.

My wandering alone through mountain retreats
Is service pleasing the dakinis.[13]
This holy dharma free from narcissism
Is service to the teachings of the Buddha.

This practice which will continue as long as I live
Is a gift to sentient beings who are without protector.

This exertion without concern for sickness or death
Is the broom that sweeps away the karma of evil deeds and
    obscurations.

This austerity of rejecting sinful food
Is the beneficial condition that gives rise to experience and
    realization.

Through practice, I repay the kindness of the father guru.
Lord guru, please protect this son with your kindness.
Grant your blessings so that this lowly one may keep to retreat.

DEVOTION TO THE GURU IS a constant reminder that we have all
the qualities necessary to become a buddha, and that our
practice is a true and complete expression of our buddha nature.
Through devotion we realize the inseparability of mind and
guru. Further, we realize phenomena as not being separate from
mind. In other words, awareness is not separate from itself; it is

not separated by the dream of ego. The object of devotion, the perfectly enlightened one, the one who was so generous as to impart the teachings to us, the one who has conquered wandering mind, the one who understands the nature of cause and effect, the nature of impermanence, and all of the things we have studied—that one is no different than our own mind. As Marpa said to Milarepa, "No matter what, we cannot be separated."

The longing that we feel for the guru is the same longing that we feel to completely free ourselves from samsara. The guru is like a lighthouse in a storm. When the waves begin to rise and the sea gets rough, there is a beacon of light. That light reveals the nature of the storm itself—the nature of the wind and water, the nature of the turbulence and agitation. At the same time, the guru is like the captain of a ship. He knows the currents; he knows how the ship moves and how much wind the sails can take. When we are terrified by the storm and afraid of drowning, the guru reminds us of our training. Since we have actually committed ourselves to this voyage, we are able to handle this situation. We do not have to feel frightened. We can trust our discipline and overcome our fear. Discursive thoughts and preoccupation with pain and pleasure become transparent.

The vision of the guru is not a product of imagination. In Milarepa's case, his vision was a reminder of Marpa's presence in his life. In the same way, remembering the dharma is like actually hearing the voice of the guru. It is the real expression of our commitment, and in that sense it comes from our own heart. Therefore devotion to the guru brings about perseverance in practice. That is what Milarepa was saying: just recalling the words, remembering the teachings and the person who embodies them, brings a shock of wakefulness. Even if that shock occurs in the length of time it takes to strike a match, that is sufficient to bring about perseverance in practice.

Remembering the guru is not some kind of wish-fulfilling fantasy. The guru reminds us of how much we have done and how much we have yet to do. In Milarepa's vision, his guru told him to practice for the benefit of others. Before he saw the vision of his guru, Milarepa thought, "Even though I have practiced, I still have conflicting thoughts which weaken my resolve." But when he saw Marpa's face and remembered the teachings he had been given, he was encouraged. He thought, "You didn't ask what my credentials were; you took a chance on me. Because of you, I can practice the dharma." It is the same for us. Without the guru, we would still just be searching for fulfillment. There would be no dharma in our life. We might be dealing in diamonds; building a new house in Vermont; going to California and getting into the health food business; going to New York and becoming a high-powered person; staying home on the farm and milking the cows. No matter what we do, it would be meaningless without the precious opportunity to practice.

Realizing that, devotion expands and increases and we become full of joy at our good fortune. The genuine guru is so generous and open that he presents the feast of dharma fearlessly. His kindness is all-encompassing and does not demand anything in return. He offers the teachings, knowing that we must make use of them ourselves. No one else can do it for us. The guru shows by his example that we can attain enlightenment through our own efforts. When we come into contact with such a person, we realize there is only one way to repay his kindness. Seeing the preciousness of what he has shown us, we long to expand our realization further and further by our practice. As Milarepa said, "Through practice, I repay the kindness of the father guru."

TWENTY

THE DAWN OF REALIZATION

Inspired, Mila put on his cotton robe, and carrying some twigs he returned to his practice cave.

Inside his cave, there were five iron atsaras,[14] who stared at him with eyes the size of saucers. One was sitting on the jetsun's bed preaching; two were listening; one was preparing food; and one was flipping through his books.

At first, Mila was shocked. Then he thought, "These must be the magical tricks of the local deity who is displeased. Although I have been dwelling in this place a long time, I have not offered any torma,[15] nor have I made even one praise. Thus I should praise this place." Then Mila sang this song in praise of the place.

E ma! This sacred ground of solitary retreat
Is the place where the victorious ones attain enlightenment.
It is the hallowed place where siddhas[16] dwelt.
This place where I dwell alone
Is the Red Rock Agate Valley Fortress of Garudas.
Above, clouds circle about.
Below, brooks gently flow.
In between, vultures sweep and soar.
Fruit trees abound.
Trees sway and dance.
Bees buzz their song.
The fragrance of flowers wafts about.
Birds chirp, a delightful sound.

At such a Red Rock Agate Valley
Birds and their young exercise their skill in flying.
Short and long-tailed monkeys exercise their skill too.
Various wild animals frolic.
I, Milarepa, exercise my skill in meditative experience.
I exercise meditative skill in the two bodhicittas.[17]
I am in harmony with the local deity of this place of solitude.
You ghosts and spirits who are gathered here,
Drink this amrita[18] of friendliness and compassion
And depart to your respective abodes.

Thus Mila sang.

The atsaras seemed to be displeased with the jetsun, and were
walking about, glancing at each other with mean looks. Then
two more atsaras joined them. Some of the seven atsaras bit
their lower lip. Some ground their teeth and clenched their
fangs. Some made mocking laughter and fierce sounds. They all
joined together and made a threatening gesture.

Mila thought, "These spirits are creating obstacles," And
therefore he recited a subjugating mantra[19] with a wrathful gaze.
They did not leave. He aroused great compassion in his heart
and though he expounded the dharma, they still did not want to
leave. Then he thought, "In Lhotrak, Marpa gave me the
transmission of all dharmas as mind. I decisively realized my
own mind as luminosity-emptiness.[20] Even if they leave, if I
cling to döns[21] and obstructing spirits as external, what is the use
of practicing this austerity?" Having realized this fearless confidence, he sang this song of possessing the confidence of
realization:

Father, victorious over the troops of the four maras,[22]
I pay homage at the feet of Marpa the Translator.

I would not call myself an ordinary man.
I am a cub of a powerful white lioness.

In the womb of my mother, I accomplished the three powers.
As a young cub, I slept in the den.
As a youth, I guarded the entrance of the den.
In my prime, I roamed the high glaciers.
No matter how intense the swirling blizzard, I have no fear.
No matter how high the precipice, I am not afraid.

I would not call myself an ordinary man.
I am a chick of the garuda, king of birds.
Already in the egg, my wings and feathers were fully developed.
As a young chick, I slept in the nest.
As a youth, I guarded the entrance of the nest.
As a great garuda in my prime, I soared through the heights of
    the sky.
No matter how great and vast the sky, I have no fear.
No matter how steep and narrow the gorge, I am not afraid.
I would not call myself an ordinary man.
I am an offspring of the great yormo fish.
In my mother's womb, my golden eyes rolled.
As a baby, I slept in the nest.
As a youth, I was foremost in swimming.
As a great fish in my prime, I explored the limits of the ocean.
No matter how giant the waves, I have no fear.
No matter how many threatening fishhooks, I am not afraid.

I would not call myself an ordinary man.
I am the son of a Kagyü guru.
Even in my mother's womb, I developed devotion.
As a child, I entered the gate of the dharma.
As a youth, I studied.
As a great meditator in my prime, I wandered in mountain
    retreats.
No matter how great the viciousness of the demons, I have no
    fear.

No matter how numerous the magical tricks of döns, I am not
    afraid.

The paws of a lion standing in the snow never freeze.
If the paws of a lion in the snow could freeze,
Accomplishment of the three powers would have little meaning.

The garuda that flies through the sky cannot fall.
If the great garuda could fall from the sky,
Fully developed wings and feathers would have little meaning.

The fish swimming in the water cannot drown.
If the great fish could be drowned by water,
Being born in the water would have little meaning.

An iron block cannot be broken by rock.
If an iron block could be broken by rock,
Smelting it would have little meaning.

I, Milarepa, am not afraid of demons.
If Milarepa were afraid of demons,
The realization of things as they are would have little meaning.

You, the assembly of demons, döns, and obstructing spirits who
    have been good enough to come here—
What a great wonder that you have come now!
Don't be in a hurry; relax and stay as long as you wish.
We shall talk and discourse at great length.
Even if you're in a hurry, by all means stay for the night.
We shall compete in the skill of the three gates,[23]
And see which is superior, the black or white dharma.[24]
You won't be able to create obstacles, nor can you return to
    your dwelling place.
Since you are unable to create obstacles, if you go home now,
Your having come here would be embarrassing.

Thus Mila sang.

Arousing the pride of the yidam, he rushed forward. The atsaras were terrified and their eyes darted about in terror. Their bodies shook so much that the whole cave began to shake, and continued until they all dissolved into one. That one turned into a whirlwind and then disappeared.

The jetsun thought, "That was Vinayaka, king of obstructing spirits, who was looking for his opportunity. Also, the wind before was his magical trick. Through the guru's kindness, he did not find his opportunity." Then, inconceivable progress in Milarepa's realization arose.

This situation created by Vinayaka, king of obstructing spirits, is called either the story "The Six Remembrances of the Guru," or the story "Red Rock Agate Valley," or else the story "Mila Gathering Wood." It has three names but one meaning. May there be virtue.

DEVOTION TO THE GURU CUTS through the lethargy and doubt we encounter in our practice. Recalling his instructions and the time we spent in his presence creates continual inspiration and energy. But inspiration is one thing; realization is another. Even though we remember the guru and his example, there is still work to be done. Realization means uncovering that which is already there. This is brought about by practice. Practice is not some kind of tool with which to manipulate or pry open buddha nature. Neither can we deceive ourselves by trying to rely on temporary experiences of realization as a kind of security.

Milarepa returned to his cave, feeling refreshed and energized. To his surprise, he found the five demons staring at him. He tried different practices to dispel negativity, but then he realized that he already understood that appearances were not separate from his own mind. He thought, "All in all, mind and phenomena are empty, shunya. Neither phenomena nor mind exist independently. In that case, what do I have to fear?" Then he sang his victorious song of realization, and ended by welcoming the demons that had come to afflict him. Milarepa said to the demons, "What a great wonder that you have come now! Don't be in a hurry; relax and stay as long as you wish. We shall talk and discourse at great length. . . . By all means stay for the night." We can welcome our fear and our doubt in the same way. That is when devotion matures into realization.

As we practice, we would like to get rid of the unpleasantness in our life; we would like to cling to happiness and joy. But suddenly we encounter an unexpected situation, just like the demons, rolling their eyes, making a mockery of us, reading our books, eating our food, growling at us. We are caught off guard, and we try to make them go away, but they don't. The notion that we can use any kind of trick or gimmick or even force to dispel negativity keeps us from realizing the nature of phenomena and the nature of our own mind. That which occurs in the realm of phenomena, in the realm of mind, occurs by itself. And moreover, that which occurs is transparent and has no solid or separate existence. We can actually subjugate obstacles by not trying to manipulate them at all. We can dispel them by inviting them as our guests. We should prepare a meal and invite our guests to sit down and partake of it. We should continually commit ourselves to following the example of those like Milarepa, who practiced the buddhadharma and understood that the essence of practice is nonaggression.

Making an offering of our practice to the guru is the best gift we can give. By continually offering, realization dawns. At that point the guru is no longer just a person; he is the principle of enlightenment that exists in all sentient beings. Therefore when we offer our body, speech, and mind to the guru, we offer to all beings, without exception. When Milarepa rushed with open arms towards the demons, he had absolutely no care for his own safety. He wasn't trying to outwit anyone; he didn't have to protect himself any more. He was just opening and offering himself.

When we are struggling on the path and wondering how we could ever do such things, we should remember to begin with what we have. We are not living in a cave in the snow mountains, but still the eight worldly winds howl around us. We are not living in solitude, but still discursive thoughts keep bothering us. We are not living on a diet of flour and water, but still we are concerned about our supper, about getting to the supermarket before it closes.

These stories of Milarepa and his life and his songs are real. When Milarepa speaks about being a vulture or a fish or the wind, or when he talks about birds flying and bees buzzing, he is not simply talking about the landscape. He is expressing the vitality of his mind and the experience of being totally one with things as they are. He is proclaiming the continuity of his realization. Milarepa stands as an example to us. In the same way, we can be an example of sanity to other sentient beings who struggle and suffer and may have never even heard of the word, *enlightenment*.

INFANT SONG
OF A SON OF THE KAGYÜ GURU

From the all-encompassing vajradhatu, indestructible
   nonthought beyond description,
From the vast dharmadhatu, the unceasing play of energy
   and light,
The dharmakaya Vajradhara takes form as the incomparable
   root guru, Chökyi Gyatso.
The five poisons and the eight worldly dharmas are
   transformed into wisdom and skillful means
Look! The aspirations and desires of sentient beings are
   fulfilled.

With unceasing devotion I prostrate to the only father guru
I offer all that is worthwhile and pleasing—the wealth of all
   the universes
I confess to lingering in the grip of samsara
I rejoice in your boundless generosity.

Please continue to turn the wheel of dharma
Remain with us in your undefiled splendor
May all sentient beings attain enlightenment
And may I never rest until samsara is thoroughly emptied.

Dharma brothers and sisters entering the immutable path,
Feeble as we are, we still have eyes and ears

Fickle as we are, we still have an empty heart
Arrogant as we are, we still have intrinsic awareness.

My friends, but for a flash of lightning there could be
    perpetual darkness
Look at the precious gem, the guru, and see the Buddha
    himself
In the brilliant mandala of suchness,
Receive his instructions with discipline and delight.

May all beings attain unsurpassable joy
May all beings be prosperous
May the victorious guru ignite the blazing fire of ultimate
    wisdom.

In order to be a good student, it is necessary to forget about
your self-importance. How to proceed is to consider everything
that emanates from the guru as definite instruction, whether it
seems mundane or profound. How to continue is to act on
instruction immediately, without self-conscious deliberation of
analysis. How to sustain your effort is to have undiminished faith
in the power of the lineage as the real expression of truth. This is
my advice according to my own experience. I wish you all great
success.

ÖSEL TENDZIN
21 March 1980

NOTES TO "THE STORY
OF RED ROCK AGATE VALLEY"

1. Sanskrit words meaning "homage to the guru."

2. A male practitioner.

3. An honorific term for a highly respected teacher.

4. The meditative transmission taught especially by the Kagyü school. In the state of mahamudra, all experiences are transformed into prajna and skillful means, which in turn manifest as the vivid and energetic display of enlightened mind.

5. A bird of Indian mythology that is said to hatch fully grown, and is therefore used as a symbol of awakened mind.

6. Tantra means continuity and refers to the continuity of the path, in which the attainment of enlightenment, based on the ground of innate wakefulness, is brought to fruition by the practices that overcome confusion. Here, tantra also refers to the root texts of the vajrayana and the practices they describe.

7. Literally, abhisheka means annointment or empowerment. It is a formal ceremony of transmission in which a student of the vajrayana is empowered by his vajra master to perform a particular practice.

8. An important collection of teachings of the anuttara yoga tantra class. Hevajra was the yidam of Marpa Lotsawa.

9. A synonym for "oral instruction lineage."

10. This term refers to the six yogic practices as well as their fruitions, which were taught to Marpa by Naropa. They are a central part of the advanced teachings transmitted by the Kagyü lineage down to the present day.

11. A meditation deity in the vajrayana. In this case, deity does not refer to an existing personage, but to the embodiment of the practition-

er's buddha nature. By identifying with a particular yidam, the practitioner can discover and express his inherent wisdom.

12.   Gain and loss; fame and disgrace; praise and blame; pleasure and pain.

13.   A wrathful or semi-wrathful female yidam, symbolizing compassion, prajna, and shunyata.

14.   A demon.

15.   A sculpture made of *tsampa* (roasted barley flour) and butter, traditionally designed as an offering.

16.   A term for an enlightened master in the vajrayana tradition. Siddha connotes one whose realization brings about the ability to utilize the magical possibilities of the phenomenal world.

17.   There are two types of bodhicitta: absolute and relative. Absolute bodhicitta is indivisible emptiness and compassion—radiant, unshakeable, and impossible to conceptualize. Relative bodhicitta, which arises from a glimpse of absolute bodhicitta, is the aspiration to practice the mahayana path and deliver all sentient beings from samsara.

18.   A blessed substance, containing liquor and relics, which aids the yogin in intoxicating the duality between samsara and nirvana. This provides the means of transforming confusion into wisdom; therefore, it is called amrita, or ''anti-death.''

19.   Words or syllables that express particular energies. Mantras are a means of transforming energy through sound and speech; mantra binds a situation into wakefulness.

20.   A state which is both empty of preconceptions—*shunya*—and full of brilliant presence and energy—*ösel* (Tibetan) or *prabhasvara* (Sanskrit), luminosity.

21.   A type of malevolent spirit, who tends to cause either physical or psychological disease in response to a lack of mindfulness on the part of the practitioner.

22.   The fundamental obstacles of clinging to a self, conflicting emotions, death, and seeking for pleasure.

23.   Body, speech, and mind: the three gates, or modes, through which one relates to the phenomenal world.

24.   Black dharma generally refers to confused acts based on passion, aggression, and ignorance. Here, it specifically refers to magical obstructions created by the atsaras. White dharma refers to the dharma of the Buddha, which teaches the means of overcoming ego-clinging.

INDEX

Actions
    transcendent, 62–64
    volitional, 22
Awakened
    being, 52
    heart, 52
    state of mind, 3, 8, 42, 67, 89
Awareness, 38–39, 40–41

Basic goodness, 1. *See also*
    Tathagatagarbha
Bodhicaryavatara. See *Entering the
    Practice of a Bodhisattva*
Bodhicitta, 51–53, 61–62
    activity of, 52
Bodhisattva, 52–54
    path, 42, 52–53
    transcendent actions of, 62–64
    vow, 52–55, 61
Buddha, 1–3, 23–24, 28
    guru as, 69–70
    See also Three jewels of refuge
Buddhadharma, 7, 22
Buddha nature, 45, 47–48,
    51–52, 61. *See also* Tatha-
    gatagarbha
Buddhist path, 2, 3, 24
    two aspects of, 8

Commitment, 22–25
Compassion, 48
    heart of, 52
    true nature of, 59
Confidence, 21
    three types of:
        trusting confidence, 22
        longing confidence, 22–23
        lucid confidence, 23
Confusion, 10, 12, 22, 23,
    29–30, 41–42, 45

Demons, 98–100
Desire, 19, 28–29
Devotion, 77–83, 86–89,
    91–93, 98–100
Dharma, 24
Discriminating awareness. *See*
    Prajna

Ego, 11, 12, 21, 22, 29, 41–42
    eroding of, 34
Egolessness, 11–13, 34
    discovery of, 11, 38–39
Embarrassment
    as fuel for bodhisattva path,
        56, 57–58

106

Vajradhatu, a world-wide organization of meditation and study centers, was founded in 1970 by Vajracarya the Venerable Chögyam Trungpa, Rinpoche. Vajradhatu has more than sixty-five local centers throughout the United States, Canada, and Europe. These centers offer programs in the study of Buddhist philosophy and psychology and the practice of meditation. Two rural centers, Karmê-Chöling in Vermont and Rocky Mountain Dharma Center in northern Colorado, provide the opportunity to study and practice in a more contemplative environment. Nalanda Foundation was established in 1974 by Trungpa Rinpoche as a nonsectarian educational organization. Its divisions include Naropa Institute, an innovative liberal arts college, and Shambhala Training, a secular meditation program.

Information on any of the Vajradhatu centers can be obtained by writing to Vajradhatu, 1345 Spruce Street, Boulder, Colorado 80302, or directly to any of the local centers listed below. Information on Naropa Institute can be obtained by writing to the institute at 1111 Pearl Street, Boulder, Colorado 80302; and Shambhala Training can be contacted at 1745 Walnut Street, Boulder, Colorado 80302. A catalogue of cassette recordings of lectures by Ösel Tendzin is available from the Naropa Institute Bookstore, 2011 Tenth Street, Boulder, Colorado 80302.

USA

Vajradhatu
1345 Spruce Street
Boulder, Colorado 80302
(303) 444-0210

Karma Dzong
1345 Spruce Street
Boulder, Colorado 80302
(303) 444-0190

Karmê-Chöling
Star Route
Barnet, Vermont 05821
(802) 633-4417

Rocky Mountain Dharma Center
Route 1
Livermore, Colorado 80536
(303) 440-0552

Dharmadhatus:

3179 Peachtree Road
Atlanta, Georgia 30305
(404) 262-2627

1702 South Fifth Street
Austin, Texas 78704
(512) 443-3263

2288 Fulton Street
Berkeley, California 94704
(415) 841-3242

32 Elmwood Avenue
Burlington, Vermont 05401
(802) 658-6795

169 Upland Road
Cambridge, Massachusetts 02145
(617) 354-7528

3340 North Clark Street
Chicago, Illinois 60657
(312) 472-7771

2329 Lincoln Street
Columbia, South Carolina 29201
(803) 779-2969

361 Transylvania Parkway
Lexington, Kentucky 40508
(606) 252-1116

2853 West Seventh Street
Los Angeles, California 90005
(213) 738-1909

5793 Commerce Lane
Miami, Florida 33143
(305) 443-1232

49 East 21st Street
New York, New York 10010
(212) 673-7340

25 Main Street
Northampton, Massachusetts 01060
(413) 584-3956

156 University Avenue
Palo Alto, California 94301
(415) 325-6437

2020 Sanson Street
Philadelphia, Pennsylvania 19103
(215) 568-6070

1819 Jackson Street
San Francisco, California 94109
(415) 776-0502

7109 Woodlawn Avenue, N.E.
Seattle, Washington 98115
(206) 522-2199

1424 Wisconsin Avenue, N.W.
Washington, D.C. 20007
(202) 338-7090

CANADA

Vajradhatu Canada
P.O. Box 2141, Station M
Halifax, Nova Scotia B3J 3B7
(902) 429-2033

Dharmadhatus:

219, 8631 109th Street
Edmonton, Alberta T6G 1E7
(403) 432-1788

5311 Avenue DuParc
Montreal, Quebec H2V 4G9
(514) 279-9115

555 Bloor Street, West
Toronto, Ontario M5S 1Y6
(416) 535-5882

3285 Heather Street
Vancouver, British Columbia V5Z 3K4
(604) 874-8420

EUROPE

Vajradhatu Europe
Dharmahaus Vogelsberg
Kirchweg 5
6315 Muche 1
West Germany
49-6400-1747

Dharmadhatus:

Ruysdaelkade 63
1072 AK
Amsterdam, Holland
Netherlands
020-79-47-53

Fleischmarkt 16
A-1010
Wien, Austria
0222-52-72-46

The text of this book is set in Perpetua,
developed by Eric Gill in 1928.
Perpetua resulted from the private press revival
and is a translation into type
of Gill's sharply carved lettering.

Designed by Julia Runk.
Set by WESType, Boulder, Colorado.
Printed and bound by Fairfield Graphics,
Fairfield, Pennsylvania.